A World of Change

A CITY AT WAR

Oxford 1642–6

Tony Kelly
History Department, Dragon School, Oxford

Rosemary Kelly
Head of History, Headington School, Oxford

Series Editor: Rosemary Kelly

How to use this book 2
Setting the scene: the two sides   3
Oxford on the eve of war 5
The King arrives 13
The city at war 17
People at war 27
Roundhead victory 40
Time chart of the Civil War 48
Find out more for yourself 50
Index 51

There are two good reasons for finding out about the story of Oxford in the English Civil War between Royalists and Parliamentarians.

The first reason is the fact that Oxford played a very important part in this war. As fighting began in earnest in 1642 the King made Oxford his headquarters, and spent most of his time there. Four years later, in 1646, the city's final surrender to Parliament meant that the war was over.

The second is that the experiences of the ordinary people who lived in Oxford were not so very different from those of people in the rest of the country. So by finding out about what happened to some of them, we can build up a more general picture. Of course we have to be careful about this: everyone who lived through the Civil War had their own individual experiences, and where they lived made a great difference to what happened to them. However, the story of the city which became the Royalist capital is an important one, and it gives us many clues about what to look for in other places.

Stanley Thornes (Publishers) Ltd

How to use this book

The story told in this book is a true one, and is based on several different kinds of evidence.

Written evidence includes descriptions, letters and diaries by people who were alive at the time, and spent at least part of the war in Oxford. When you use this kind of evidence, you must be cautious and critical. It is important to find out as much as possible about the person who has written it: their beliefs may make them very one-sided witnesses. They may not have been actually present at the events they describe; or, if they were, they may not have seen everything that happened. If they seem to have relied on gossip, then you must decide how much truth there is in that. Even official records can be one-sided. The records of Oxford University and the City Council give their own viewpoint, and so do official announcements by both sides. Propaganda produced to win support often does not attempt to be truthful, though we may still be able to learn a good deal from it.

Pictorial evidence can tell us a great deal too. Portraits can bring a person to life, and we can learn how people saw themselves by how they chose to be painted. Pictures produced cheaply to be sold to ordinary people are full of information about everyday life and attitudes. Maps can tell us about the places where important events happened: the maps produced in Oxford during the war are full of information, though once again we have to be careful about their accuracy. Modern maps are helpful too, and so are photographs. It is even better if you can actually see the places which come into this story.

All these different kinds of evidence are important, and if they are pieced together it is often possible to understand what really happened.

There are two other important things to remember. First, there are gaps in this story. Space in a book is always limited, and the authors have had to choose what to include. Evidence is missing too. For instance, most of what happened in wartime Oxford was described by the supporters of one side, the Royalists. Yet there were plenty of Parliamentarians in Oxford too. Another gap is the experiences of women in the city. There were probably as many women as men in the city most of the time (though they would have been outnumbered when the full garrison was there), but we have been able to include only a little of what they were thinking, feeling, and doing. Perhaps, when you have finished this book, you may be able to think of some reasons for these two gaps. You may notice other missing links yourself.

Finally, remember that in the story of the Civil War, which had such an effect on the way Britain developed, we all tend to have our likes and dislikes. The authors of this book have tried hard to be fair. You must decide whether they have succeeded; but you must watch your own feelings too.

The cover picture is part of 'The Siege of Oxford' by de Wyck, by courtesy of the Earl of Dartmouth, and the Museum of Oxford.

This scene of the siege of Oxford in 1646 was painted some years after the war by a Dutch artist. He probably had de Gomme's map (see page 17) in front of him as he worked, but did not actually visit Oxford, as he has made the surrounding countryside much more hilly than it actually is. However, the picture helps us to imagine what the closing stages of the story in this book were like. You can see the whole picture in the Museum of Oxford in St Aldates.

Setting the scene: the two sides

Some of the contemptuous or scornful nicknames which the two sides gave each other are often used in this book, and it is important to understand them. They help to explain the much bigger problem of why the two sides divided.

Cavalier This was the best known nickname for Royalists who fought for the King; they did not always agree with his actions, but they were loyal, and felt that Parliament had gone too far in limiting his powers, and attacking the Church of England, of which he was head. 'Cavalier' meant a haughty, cruel horseman, who slaughtered and looted, but Royalists grew to like the name, and Charles I said:

> The valour of Cavaliers hath honoured that name . . . it signifying no more than a gentleman serving his King on horseback.

Roundhead This was the nickname for Parliamentarians; most of them felt they had been forced into a war they did not want, by a King whose promise to share power with Parliament they could not trust. Queen Henrietta Maria was said to have looked out at the hostile mob of Londoners outside the palace of Whitehall, just before the war started. She saw so many short-haired London apprentices that she called them 'Roundheads'. Gentlemen in the seventeenth century wore their hair long, so a great many Parliamentarians, including Fairfax and Cromwell, were certainly not 'Roundheads', but the name stuck. Like the Cavaliers, the Roundheads made the best of their nickname: 'Though we be roundheaded, we be not hollow-hearted.'

Puritan Many Parliamentarians were Puritans. They were people who wanted to 'purify' the Church of England, because they firmly believed that the King and his Archbishop, William Laud, were making it much too like the Catholic Church. Though they found it difficult to agree on what should be done to stop this, most of them feared the power of the bishops, and wanted more say in church matters. They relied on the Bible, and believed that preaching would spread the word of God, rather than services laid down in the Prayer Book. They hated pictures and statues in churches and did not like kneeling, because they felt that all this encouraged superstition and 'idolatry' (worship of idols). Most Puritans disliked their nickname – perhaps because it *was* a nickname.

Papist This was the traditional nickname that most English people used for Catholics. The Protestant martyrs of Mary I's reign, the Spanish Armada and the Gunpowder Plot were old history by 1642, but few had forgotten them, and Catholics were seen as traitors, loyal to England's enemies abroad, and above all to a foreign Pope. Most English Catholics just wanted to live quietly, with freedom to practise their faith, but to many of their subjects Charles I and his Catholic queen, Henrietta Maria, seemed to be much too sympathetic to 'Popery' and 'Popish' practices. So the nickname was used with added venom, and Papists were blamed for every danger and threat.

■ We often use nicknames today, not always kindly. Can you think of any which are used because of hatred or fear, like the Civil War ones?

Charles I (1625–49)

The King whose reign bitterly divided his subjects, by Van Dyck

Charles I became King when he was a young man of 25, and his reign ended when he was publicly executed in 1649, three years after the final surrender of Oxford. He was a dignified and artistic man, who was a sincere and loyal believer in the Church of England, of which he was head. He was also a faithful and loving husband to his French Queen, Henrietta Maria, who was a Catholic and had a great deal of influence over him. Although he had good qualities, Charles failed to understand his subjects, especially the powerful ruling classes; many of them resented the way he demanded taxes without their consent, and feared that he was giving too much favour to Catholics. He became isolated in his well-ordered and civilised court. Since he believed that his power was given him by God, he saw no need to explain or alter his actions, however many people opposed him. 'A subject and a sovereign are clear different things', he once said.

These three heads were painted by the great court artist, Anthony Van Dyck, some years before the war, though the King probably still looked like this when he was in wartime Oxford. The leading sculptor of the day, Bernini, who worked in Rome, had been given the task of carving a bust (head and shoulders statue) of Charles. Van Dyck painted the three heads to be sent to the sculptor to work from, since the King could not go to Rome himself. So it is as if we can walk round Charles and view him from several different angles. What is your impression of him?

Oxford on the eve of war

Sir John Byron, by William Dobson

Lord Saye and Sele, by an unknown artist

In the late summer of 1642, two visitors came to Oxford.

On the night of 28 August, Sir John Byron clattered into the city streets with a detachment of Royalist cavalry, causing considerable alarm. His visit was short; but when he left on 8 September, things did not stay quiet for long. Two days later, Parliamentary troops marched in, and the Puritan nobleman, Lord Saye and Sele, arrived to take command. He too did not stay long, but many of the citizens and scholars had begun to arm themselves . . .

It was a confusing and dangerous time for everyone in Oxford. All over the country it was the same. The terrible prospect of civil war was beginning to divide people of the same nation, and set families and neighbours against each other. A great many just tried to keep out of the quarrel. For the citizens of Oxford, that was going to be very difficult. Like many other people in 1642, they lived in a divided city.

The University

Oxford had really been a divided city for centuries. The rich and powerful university was quite separate from the city, and dominated the townspeople's lives in many ways. It controlled all the city's busy and profitable markets, as well as alehouses and inns. It owned a great many of the houses and shops where the citizens lived and worked. Once a year, the Mayor and chief citizens had to pay a fine and walk in procession to the university church for a special service in memory of sixty scholars who had been killed in a terrible riot three hundred years before. (However, townspeople had been killed as well, and no one really knew who had started the trouble.)

In the seventeenth century, the university was still growing. New colleges were founded; others were improving their existing buildings. Sir Thomas Bodley enlarged and improved the already famous library, and it was renamed 'The Bodleian' after him.

The organisation of the University

The Chancellor was head of the university. He was usually someone well known and important, and rarely lived in Oxford.

The Vice-Chancellor acted for the Chancellor when he was not in Oxford.

The Colleges were where the students lived. Their buildings were arranged round courtyards called quadrangles. They were rich in land, valuable books, and gold and silver plate (dishes, plates, and cups used at table or in church).

The dons, or *Fellows*, were the teachers. They lived in the colleges, and looked after:

The Scholars or students. They started their studies aged about seventeen, and learnt Greek, Latin and Theology (religion). After about three years, they gained a degree, and became Masters of Arts. They were usually quite well-off, and became country gentlemen, lawyers or clergymen.

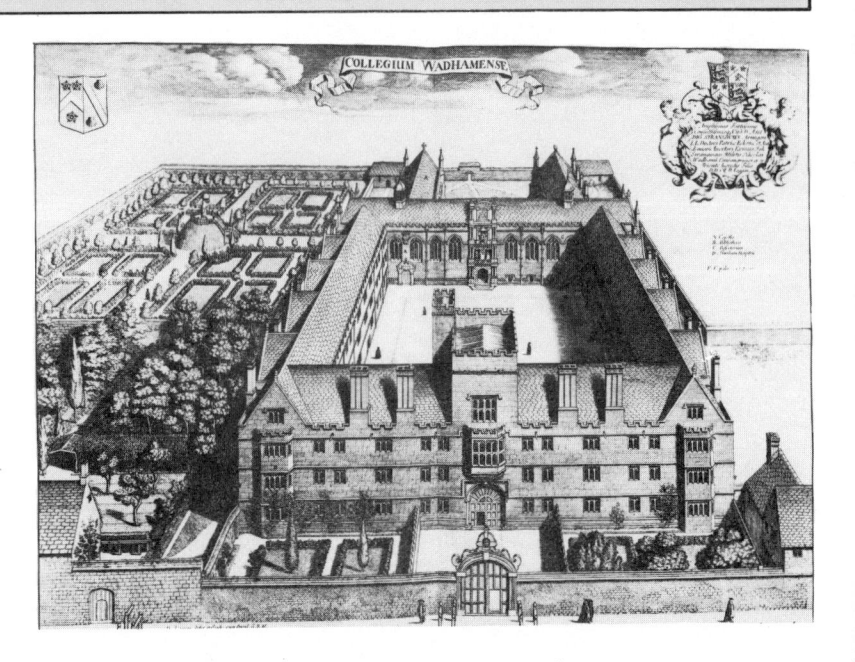

Wadham College, showing a typical quadrangle, round which the dons and scholars lived

King Charles I took a special interest in the university, and he made sure it was organised to train loyal supporters. His Archbishop of Canterbury, William Laud, was very active in carrying out the King's wishes in Oxford in the years just before the war. Laud was Chancellor of the university for a time, and he hoped to influence many of the scholars to help him in his other aim: a better organised church, with powerful bishops, and dignified, beautiful services. He and the King disliked and distrusted Puritans, and the Puritans felt the same about Laud.

Charles I was not always very successful in winning support from his subjects. However, in Oxford University his hopes were fulfilled. Almost all the dons and scholars were Royalist in 1642.

Some of Archbishop Laud's Rules for the University

1. Scholars had to pass examinations in order to gain a degree. Formerly, all a student had to do was to attend lectures and formal debates, and do some written work.

2. Scholars were not to 'idle and wander about the City, nor be seen standing or loitering about the townsmen or workmen's shops'. They were not to go into inns, or shops that sold wine or other drink, or tobacco.

3. Playing cards or dice for money was not allowed. Football was forbidden within the university, and so was hunting 'with hounds, ferrets, or nets' which might cause trouble to others.

4. Dress was to be sober. Scholars had to 'abstain from that absurd and assuming practice of walking publicly in boots'. Long hair was forbidden, and swords, daggers, bows and arrows and guns were not to be carried. (Look at the portraits in this book to find what was fashionable wear for men.)

William Laud (1573–1645), after Van Dyck

Archbishop of Canterbury, and one of the King's chief advisers before the war. He was loyal and hard-working but also tactless and high-handed. He became very unpopular, and in 1641 was imprisoned by Parliament. He was executed in 1645, as the war came to an end.

1 How did Archbishop Laud want the scholars to behave?
2 What kind of things did the scholars obviously enjoy doing?

Dons and scholars in Merton College

The dons are wearing academic dress (gowns and mortar boards). You can see the scholars did not spend all their time studying — they are playing a ball game called 'Fives' against the wall. Who do you think the men carrying sacks in the foreground are?

A royal visit

Part of the Canterbury Quadrangle in St Johns College — one of Archbishop Laud's gifts to the university

Laud had been a student there, and later became President (head) of the College. The quadrangle is built of honey-coloured stone, with marble pillars. It is dominated by this statue of Charles I carved by a well-known sculptor, Hubert Le Sueur. Facing it on the opposite side of the quadrangle is one of the Queen, Henrietta Maria. Laud paid for all this himself, and encouraged other building in Oxford.

In August, 1635, King Charles I came to Oxford to inspect the new quadrangle (see above). With him came his Queen, Henrietta Maria, his sixteen-year-old nephew, Prince Rupert, and large numbers of courtiers. Although of course no one realised it, the next time most of these people came to Oxford, it would be to a very different, wartime city.

Three days of elaborate and expensive entertainment were organised by Archbishop Laud. All the important people in the university took part, and so did many of the scholars. One of the events was a vast banquet in St Johns College, on which Laud spent £2266 — about half the cost of building the quadrangle. This large sum was obviously not enough, because various noblemen and friends contributed *extra* supplies including two fat oxen, two stags, seventy fat sheep, and twenty brace (pairs) of pheasants. There were also 'baked meats', probably some kind of sweet pastry, which were models of archbishops, bishops, and dons, 'wherein the King and courtiers took much content'.

Archbishop Laud does not seem to have enjoyed it all very much. He wrote with relief to friends that he had returned home 'after my weary expenseful business in Oxford . . . Tis most true, the matters are small in themselves, but to me they are great, and I am most heartily glad they are over'. However, he was happy about one thing: he had had to borrow a great deal of extra plate for the banquet, including some of the King's. Only two spoons were missing, and those belonged to the Archbishop.

1 What does the information on this page, and the portrait on page 7 tell you about the character and interests of Archbishop Laud?

2 Work out what you think the following groups felt about Laud's work in Oxford: *(i)* The dons;   *(ii)* The scholars.

The city

The hundred years before 1642 had been prosperous and peaceful for the city of Oxford. The population grew from 5000 to 10,000; a great deal of building went on inside and outside the city walls. Tradesmen and craftsmen did well; but the old resentment against the university and the way it controlled their affairs remained. Puritan preachers had a large following, and many townspeople disliked Archbishop Laud's religious reforms. They had a strong suspicion that he was really a Papist, and particularly objected to the new porch which his chaplain had built in front of the old university church of St Marys in the High Street. It had statues of the Virgin and Child, and two angels, which they considered shockingly Popish.

As war approached in 1642, feelings were running high in the city streets. Undoubtedly, most citizens supported Parliament. Anthony Wood, the diarist, described what was happening: 'This year saw many troubles and tokens of approaching ruin'. Puritan preachers were behaving 'insolently against the scholars', and were trying 'to turn all things topsy turvy'. They openly preached rebellion, and the townspeople were ready to 'tumult and rise against the scholars. They had meetings every night at Carfax either to confront . . . authority or to embrace novelties and reports that daily and hourly came from London concerning the affairs of the nation'.

The new porch of St Marys Church

Notice how important the unpopular statues were in the design of the porch.

Look at the information about Anthony Wood on page 47.

1 It is well known that he was a loyal member of the university. Find at least one example in this account which shows this.

2 How reliable a witness was he for the events in Oxford in 1642?

3 What do you think is meant by 'novelties and reports' from London?
What would the reports be about?
What kind of people would probably bring this news to Oxford?

The city and its leaders

The City Council ran the affairs of the city. It made great efforts to see that the streets were kept clean, and to prevent fire amongst the crowded wooden houses. It tried hard to weaken the university's control over the townspeople's affairs, but was not very successful. The City Council was elected by the 600 freemen of the city.

The Mayor and Aldermen were the city's leaders, and were chosen from the City Council.

Trades and occupations in the city of Oxford

The lists of freemen who had the right to choose the City Council still exist, and as they give the occupation of each freeman, they tell us a great many of the trades and occupations at this time. They do not include every trade in Oxford. For instance, there are no printers, bookbinders, and booksellers. Yet the book trade was a very important one. Who would have been the best customers?

However, we can get a good idea of how people earned their living. Use the list of occupations given below to make a chart. Arrange them in boxes, under the headings given in capital letters. By each occupation, you could draw a small picture showing either what was produced, or what tools were used.

Some definitions are given. You could use a dictionary for any others you do not know.

FOOD AND DRINK
BUILDING
OTHER HOUSEHOLD NEEDS
MEDICAL CARE

TRANSPORT
CLOTHING AND SHOES –
include all leather-workers
ANY OTHER TRADES

Butcher
Hosier
Carpenter
Joiner
Brewer
Cutler
Fuller
Dyer
Glazier – someone who puts glass in windows
Miller
Plumber – at that time, this meant someone who worked in lead, used for pipes and roofs
Furrier
Clockmaker
Boatman

Capper – cap maker
Barber-surgeon – barbers performed minor operations
Wheelmaker
Mercer – dealer in textiles, especially silk
'Syngingman'– many churches and chapels had choirs
Bellhanger
Shoemaker
Ostler – stableman
'Potycarie' – apothecary, chemist
Glover
Slater
Painter

Draper
Cook
Weaver
Baker
Mason
Chandler – candlemaker, who sometimes sold soap, oil, and paint
Woollen draper
Carver
Fishmonger
Haberdasher
Blacksmith
Tanner
Wagonmaker
Armourer
Physician
Chapman – pedlar

■ Which of these people would be likely to do well from the university? Put a star by them on your chart.

The two visitors

And so it was into a divided city that Sir John Byron rode with his Royalist cavalry on 28 August 1642. The townsmen tried to close the gates, but the Vice-Chancellor, the Mayor, and other Royalist supporters greeted Sir John and his troops at Magdalen Bridge with cries of 'Welcome, gentlemen!' However, according to Wood, his arrival caused alarm:

> insomuch that everyone being in a maze, did not know whether to stand to their arms or abscond [run away], but at length it being known which party they were, the scholars closed with [joined] them, and were joyful for their coming.

But when Byron's troopers started to break down the great arched stone bridge between Oxford and Botley to convert it into a drawbridge and so make the city safer from attack by Parliamentary forces, many of the citizens were not pleased and tried to stop them. Nor did they approve when Royalist supporters tried to drown a Puritan sermon being preached to the Mayor by 'striking up drums'.

The arrival of these troops obviously gave a good excuse for hooliganism, as John Smyth, Member of Parliament for Oxford City (and no Royalist) discovered when he and his wife were beaten up by soldiers and scholars. Walter Cave, mercer and brewer, was another unhappy man when late one night his house was searched by the Vice-Chancellor and Mayor who suspected him of Parliamentarian sympathies. It was a worrying time; and it is not surprising that the City Council, on 20 August, had already laid down that 'in these tumultuous times, it is necessary that every citizen should have arms to defend this city and themselves . . .'

However, on 8 September, Byron and his men left, taking with them one hundred scholars who had volunteered to join the King's army. Byron was a typical dashing Cavalier officer. Someone at the time described him as the kind of soldier who would 'engage the enemy when he needed not'. Four months after his visit to Oxford, the Royalist news-sheet reported that in a night attack at Burford, Byron had received 'a blow on the face from a pole-axe . . . wherewith he was in danger to have fallen from his horse', but he recovered, survived the war, and lived until 1652.

A Cavalier trooper

1 Look carefully at the portrait of Byron on page 5, and find a clue which tells whether it was painted before or after his visit to Oxford.

2 What might the Mayor and Vice-Chancellor have been looking for in Walter Cave's house?

3 Write an imaginary letter from Byron to the King giving his opinion of the citizens of Oxford, and how they behaved during his visit.

The second visitor to Oxford was a very different person. Lord Saye and Sele was a thorough Puritan and Parliament man, and was so shrewd and cautious that he was nicknamed 'Old Subtlety'. His home, Broughton

Castle, was only twenty miles from Oxford, and it had been a secret meeting place for important Parliamentarian leaders before the war broke out.

The university made plans to resist him. Trenches were dug, Magdalen Bridge was barricaded, stones were hauled to the top of Magdalen Tower ready to be hurled down on any attackers, and Dr Pink, the Warden (head) of New College, mustered the scholars and drilled them in New College quadrangle. This proved too much for some of the young people, as Wood tells us:

> It being a novel matter, there was no holding of the schoolboys in their school in the cloister from seeing and following them . . . and some of them were so besotted with the training and activity and gaiety therein . . . that they could never be brought to their books again. It was a great disturbance to the youth of the city.

But none of this prevented Lord Saye and his men from occupying the city, and he was 'strongly pressed' by the townspeople to hold it for Parliament. This he would not do, perhaps because of the danger involved in trying to defend this divided city. However, he took the weapons away from the university, armed the citizens, sent Dr Pink to prison in London, and removed a quantity of plate from some of the colleges.

As he had been a scholar at the university himself, he did not want to do any damage, but he was anxious to protect it against Popery, 'so lately increased there' and he ordered several 'popish books and pictures' to be burned in the streets. His troopers fired at the statue of the Virgin on the porch of St Marys which was so unpopular with the Puritans. The Virgin's head was broken off; many townspeople were delighted, but members of the university were horrified.

■ Look back at the portrait of Lord Saye and Sele on page 5. What differences do you see in character and appearance between him and Sir John Byron?

Lord Saye also ordered the destruction of what he thought were Popish pictures in the chapel of Trinity College, but the President, Dr Kettell, pretended no one ever noticed them. 'Truly, my lord', he said, 'we regard them no more than a dirty dishcloth'. The pictures were not touched.

On 20 September, Lord Saye and his men left. They went to join a Parliamentary army gathering to the north of Oxford. In just over a month, the uneasy peace would be shattered by the first great battle of the Civil War – Edgehill, fought only thirty miles away.

The Battle of Edgehill

The King arrives

Why choose Oxford?

After the Battle of Edgehill, which was really a victory for neither side, Charles's first and most urgent task was to find a headquarters for his army and his Court because the obvious choice — London, the capital — had been in the control of Parliament since the beginning of 1642.

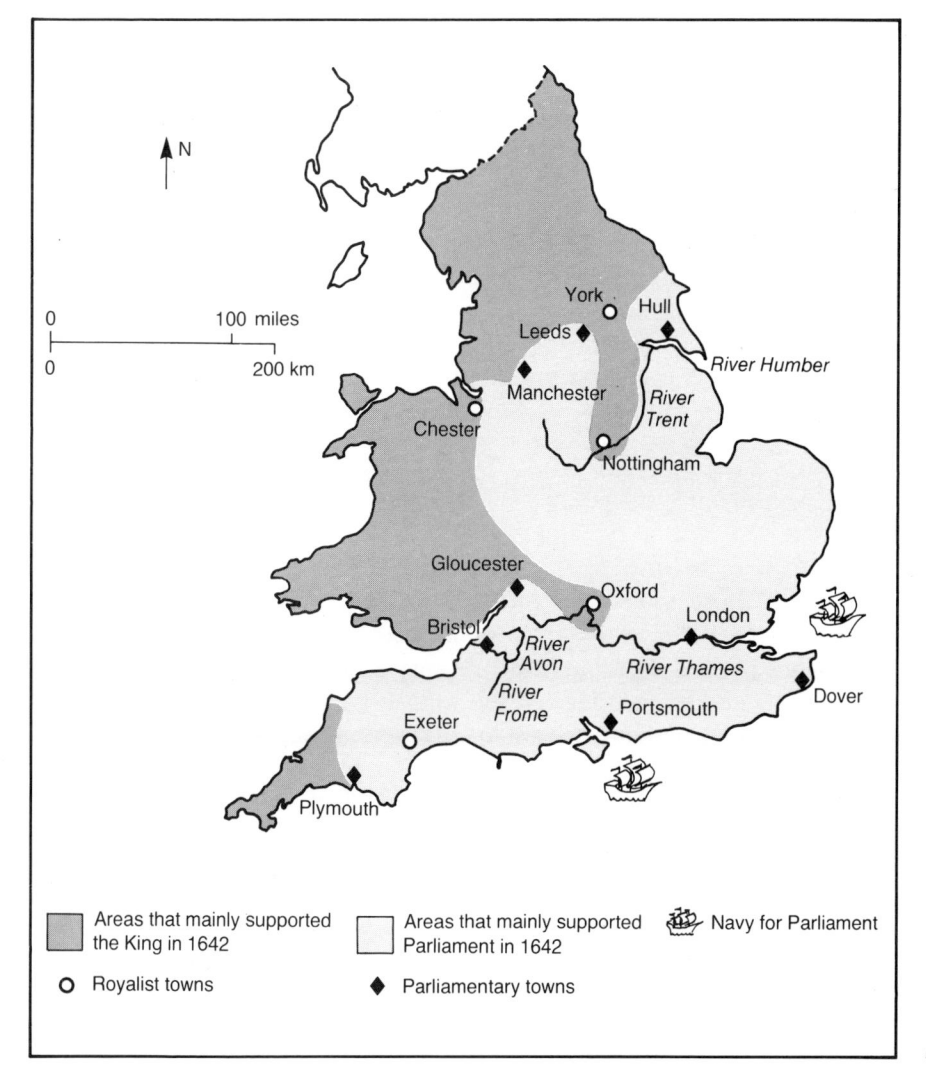

England and Wales in 1642

Look at the map on the previous page and think about the points below.

A good headquarters should be:

A In a reasonably central position, so that it is within striking distance of enemy movements and bases particularly London, which Charles had to capture if he wanted to win the war.

B Not too difficult to defend from enemy attack, i.e. it should have artificial defences such as walls, or natural defences, such as rivers.

C Positioned in friendly territory, where the inhabitants are more or less on your side.

D Able to receive reinforcements and supplies by river or sea.

E A good centre for communications, i.e. not placed in a lonely area where roads are few and far between.

F Large and rich enough to accommodate and feed a considerable number of people.

Instead of Oxford, Charles might have thought about the three following places as possibilities for his headquarters:

York In Charles's time, it was considered the northern capital of England. In March 1642 Charles was there with his court. Its port was Hull, which was controlled by Parliament. Two of the great families in the neighbourhood were divided in their loyalties. The Saviles were for the King, the Fairfax family for Parliament. There was sometimes quarrelling in the streets of the city by the different supporters. In the whole of the surrounding area, the Earl of Newcastle was a very powerful Royalist. Many of the local people were frightened of an Irish Catholic invasion in support of the King. The city had four miles of stout walls and there were two rivers to help in its defence.

Nottingham The townspeople's loyalties were divided. It was a prosperous, busy town with a population of about 5000. The Humber estuary could be reached by the navigable River Trent, but that was controlled by the Parliamentary stronghold of Hull. The town commanded an important bridge in the Midlands, and was in a very central position. Charles had raised his standard there in August 1642.

Bristol At the beginning of the war, it was in the hands of Parliament, and it would have to be captured. It had a wall and ditch five miles long, protecting one side and studded with forts for mounting cannon. The Rivers Avon and Frome provided additional defence, as well as a castle. In spite of the Parliamentary garrison, the citizens were on the whole more for the King than for Parliament. It was an important city – the second greatest seaport in the country.

Copy out the table on the page opposite, and give a mark out of five for each of the points A—F. Use pages 6, 7 and 9 and the map on page 13 to make up your mind what Oxford should score. After you have totalled up the score for each city, you can decide whether you think that Charles was right to choose Oxford.

	A	B	C	D	E	F	TOTAL
YORK							
NOTTINGHAM							
BRISTOL							
OXFORD							

It is interesting to note that as late as 1645, Parliament issued orders to their General Fairfax:

> that Oxford shall be *presently* besieged, having found by experience for three years past that the advantage of that place situate in the heart of the kingdom hath enabled the enemy to have ill influence upon this *City* and Counties adjoining, and to infest all other parts.

immediately

London

A ceremonial entry

On 29 October 1642 Anthony Wood noted:

> the King's majesty, toward the evening came from Edgehill . . . to Oxford in at the North gate on horse back, with his army of foot men; Prince Rupert and his brother Maurice, also the young prince Charles and his brother the Duke of York came in also: they lodged at Christ Church; the footmen were billeted in and about Oxford. They came in their full march into the town, with about 60 or 70 *colours* borne before them which they had taken at the said battle of Edgehill from the Parliament's forces . . . At Christ Church the University stood to welcome his majesty.

flags

It was an encouraging entry for the King. He had already received support from the university in the form of money (£860), though Parliament had not been pleased at hearing this:

> we do order and command that the Heads and Fellows do forbear that wicked and unlawful course, and do forthwith put their plate and money into some safe place under good security, that it be not employed against the Parliament.

One month before, also, the King had written to the Mayor and Council more or less ordering them to replace with reliable councillors those who had left the city, because they were too obviously Puritan and sympathetic to the cause of Parliament. One of these men was Alderman John Nixon, Lord Saye's suggested candidate for mayor.

Whenever Charles entered a city in his kingdom, the important citizens would give him a ceremonial greeting, and the ordinary people would turn out to watch. Here he is being greeted by the Lord Mayor on his arrival in London before the war. His entry into Oxford was probably very like this.

The King's letter ran:

> We understand that there are diverse aldermen ... of our city of Oxford who many months since have gone from thence into rebellion ... whereby that town must needs be the worse governed, such ill members possessing those places. We have therefore thought it necessary to recommend it to your special care forthwith to *disenfranchise* and remove such as have thus deserved it by their absence ... and to make choice of other able and fit men to supply those places.

disenfranchise — deprive of their rights

The citizens put on a show of being loyal to the King when he arrived by presenting him with £520, but they were obviously not trusted because very soon they were disarmed; and their Member of Parliament was arrested for supporting Parliament, and for urging the citizens not to fortify the town for the King.

In November Charles and his army marched south in an attempt to take London, but they were turned back on the outskirts at Turnham Green. Charles was never again to come so close to capturing the capital; and when he reached Oxford once more on 29 November there was no doubt that it would now remain his headquarters.

The main task now was to fortify the city.

1 Look back at pages 9 and 10 to the information about the city and its trades and occupations. What reasons would some citizens have for wanting to oppose the King? What advantages would there be in cooperation? Which trades and occupations would do well out of the Royalist garrison?

2 Write a conversation in which two city councillors discuss what their answer to the King should be.

The city at war

Soldiers building defences against attack

The defences

With troops and supplies flooding into Oxford, and the King and his Court to be protected, it was essential that the city should be well defended. A Dutch engineering expert, Sir Bernard de Gomme, was called in, and he made a plan; simplified versions of this can be seen on page 21.

The old city walls and the castle were no longer much use, so de Gomme planned a series of encircling earthworks (ditches and ramparts), with those to the north of the city being particularly strong. The distance from the bottom of the ditch to the top of the rampart was about 5 metres; and stakes with sharpened points called storm poles were embedded in the rampart, projecting downwards to make it difficult for attackers to climb the sides. The ramparts were lined with turf or hurdles (interwoven sticks and twigs), and behind them there would be a firestep (a raised walkway from which a defender could view the enemy and fire his musket).

Arrangements were also made for the rivers to be flooded to provide additional defence.

1 Why do you think the earthworks to the north of the city had to be stronger than those to the south?

2 Why were the defences arranged for the most part in zigzag form?

3 Three fortified outposts are marked on the lower map on page 21. What do you think was the particular importance of Outpost 1?

4 Draw a labelled sketch of an earthwork showing firestep, rampart, ditch and storm poles. Use the description on page 17 to help you.

5 Why do you think the ramparts were lined and not left bare?

6 Now look at the picture on the previous page which shows a rampart being built (though it was not in Oxford). Explain carefully what the people on the rampart are doing. What are the people in front doing? How many of the features of your sketch of a rampart can you find in the picture? What differences can you see? What evidence can you see that this will be part of a zigzag rampart?

The work on the defences went very slowly; this was mainly because the citizens had to do it themselves, unpaid, or provide money for others to do it, and neither alternative pleased them. The King went personally to inspect progress and was also not pleased: 'whereof his majesty then took notice, and told them of it himself in the field.' His reaction was not surprising when we discover that on one occasion, although 122 citizens had been ordered to work, only 12 appeared. The students, on the other hand, were eager to help. One eye-witness said that they 'do night and day gall their hands with mattocks and shovels.'

1 Why would the students be more eager to help than the citizens?

2 Does the evidence suggest they were used to working with their hands?

Outside Oxford it was important for the King to have strong points, to protect the city and keep routes open for supplies to get through. Copy the map on page 19 and find on it the places named in the following list. Indicate, perhaps by colour, which were held by the Royalists, which by Parliament and which changed sides at different times. Emphasise by colour the course of the rivers and insert an arrow to show the direction of London, the Parliament headquarters.

For the King: Buckingham, Bletchingdon Manor, Boarstall House, Brill, Shirburn Castle, Greenland House, Compton Wynyates, Donnington Castle, Faringdon, Radcot, Gaunt House (which commanded the river crossing at Newbridge), Woodstock, Mapledurham, Burford, Rousham, Chastleton House. Captured in 1642: Banbury, Broughton Castle.

For Parliament: Aylesbury, High Wycombe, Henley, Littlecote House.

Later captured by Parliament: Abingdon, Banbury, Reading, Wallingford.

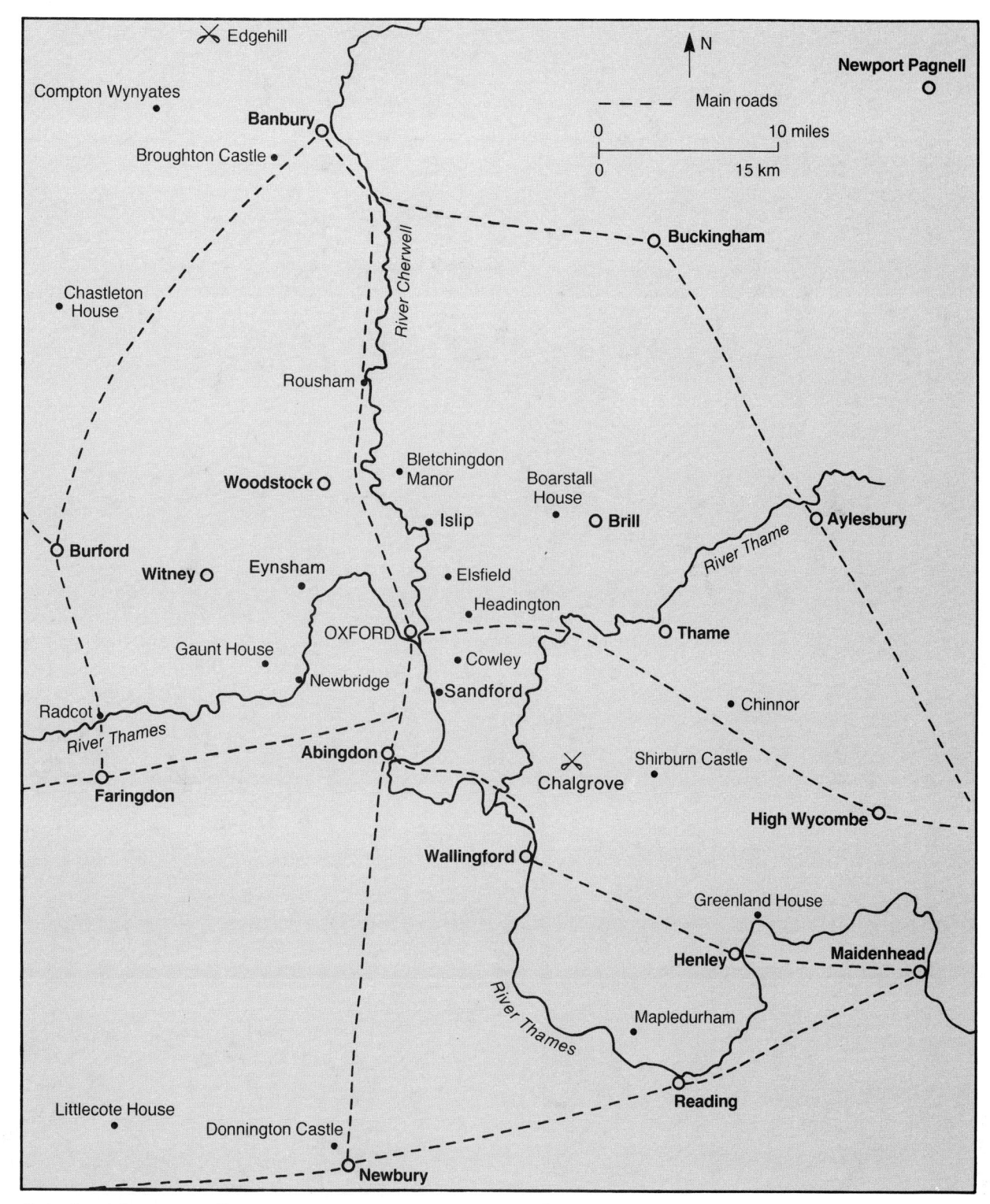

Oxford and the surrounding area

Oxford now became a garrison city. From Shotover, wood and timber were brought in for the defences (so was white clay, to make the soldiers' tobacco pipes); the infantry encamped themselves between Oxford and Wolvercote; and at Wolvercote itself a mill was established for grinding sword blades, which had been forged at Gloucester Hall. At Osney the existing mills were adapted to grinding gunpowder, and a large private house at Godstow was first fortified as an outpost and later (1645) destroyed lest it fall into Parliament's hands. (A defensive wall with loopholes for muskets can still be seen there.) Within the city itself there was great activity, as heavy guns clattered along the roads to be parked in Magdalen Grove, drawn by their teams of horses or oxen. Some of these guns weighed as much as 3.5 tonnes and had a range of $1\frac{1}{2}$ miles (about 2.5 km).

Elsewhere in the city, buildings were taken over for garrison purposes. The halls where Law, Logic, Music, Astronomy, and Rhetoric were normally studied ('The Schools') were put to use as warehouses for cloth, coal, corn and cheese, and as factories for making uniforms and army equipment such as drawbridges for the defences. At Frewin Hall a cannon foundry was set up, and the ordnance (artillery) officials installed their powder and arms magazine (storehouse) in the tower and cloister of New College. Soon word went round that metal was needed, and the lead from the Cornmarket roof was stripped for bullets, bells from some of the neighbouring churches were brought in, and citizens were told to bring their brass kitchenware to be melted down for gun-making. The citizens obviously did not like losing their saucepans and kettles: only 40 people are recorded as bringing articles in, and the total weight collected came to scarcely 350 kg.

Below right: Seventeenth-century cannons pulled by men and horses

Below: Christ Church College, taken from a Royalist book describing early events in the Civil War

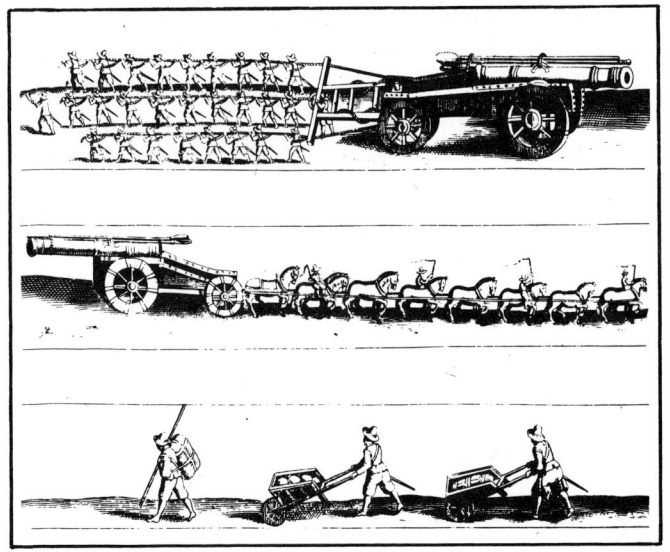

The city fortified

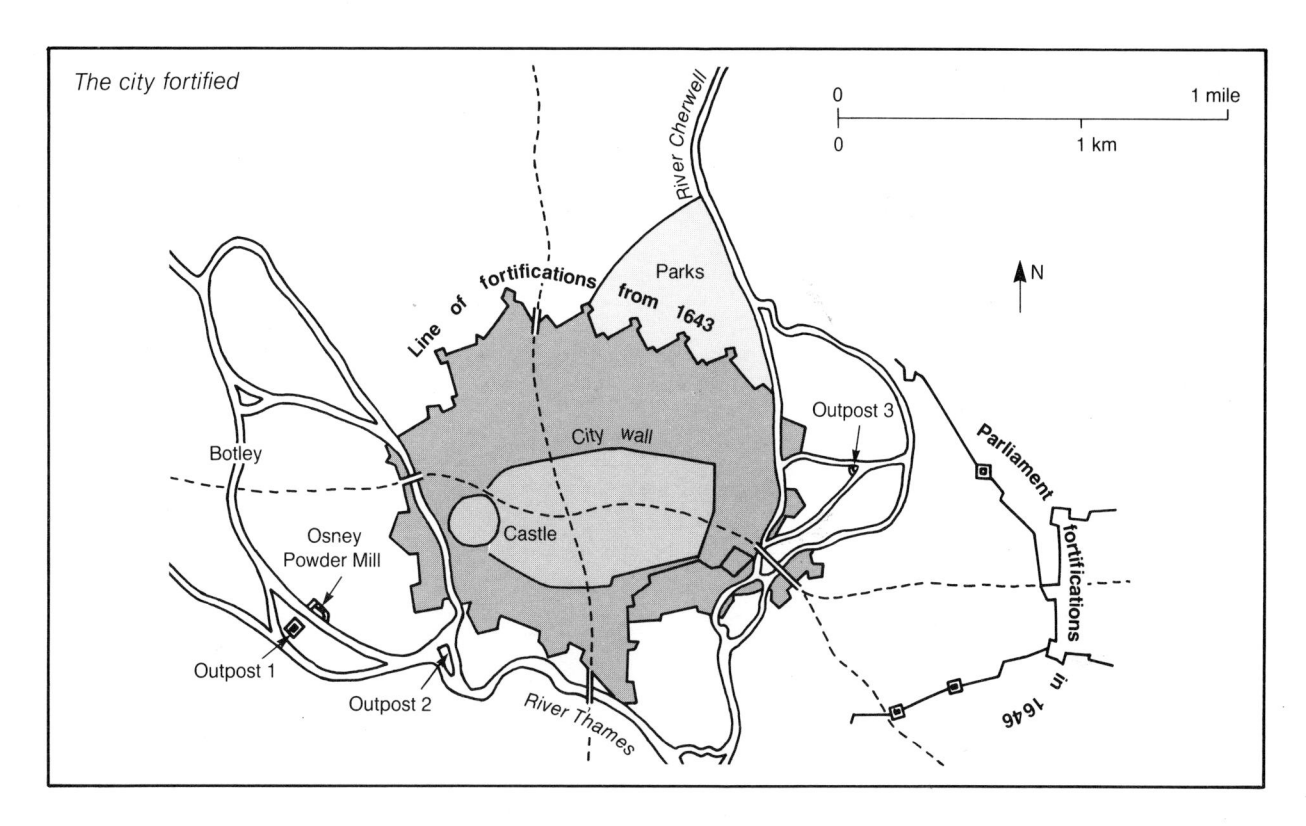

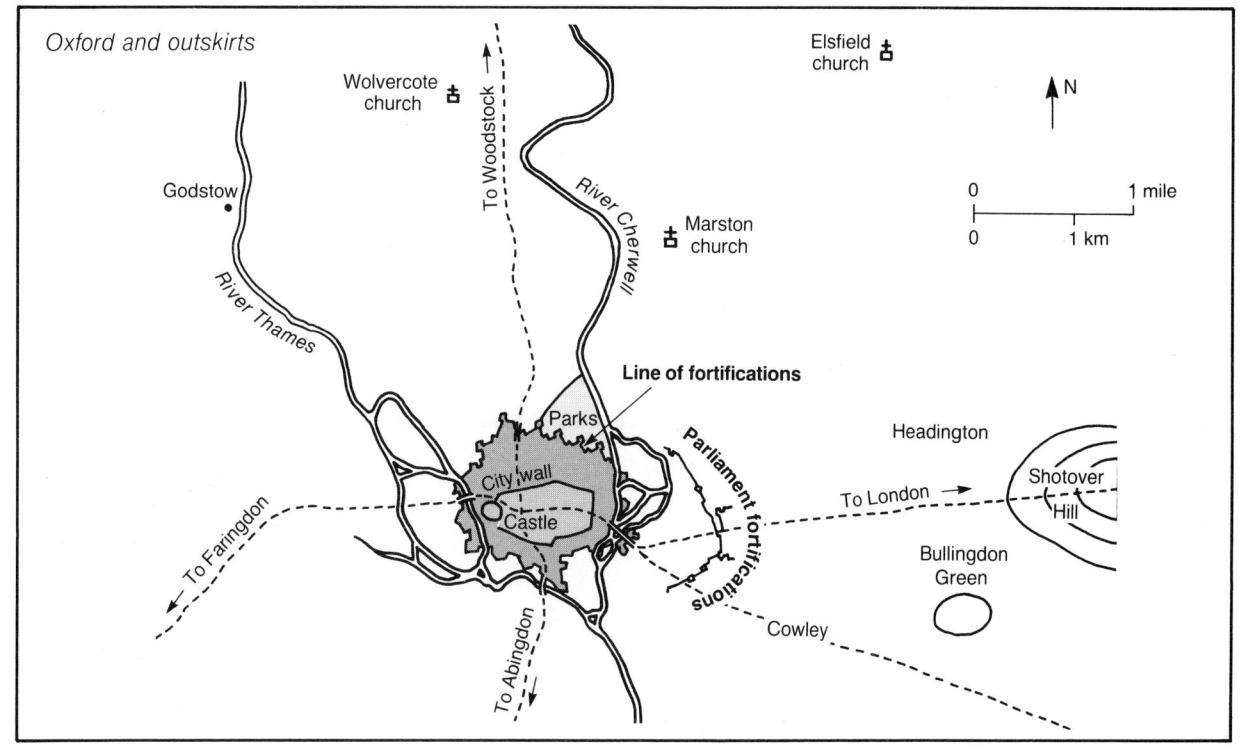

Oxford and outskirts

21

Oxford in 1643

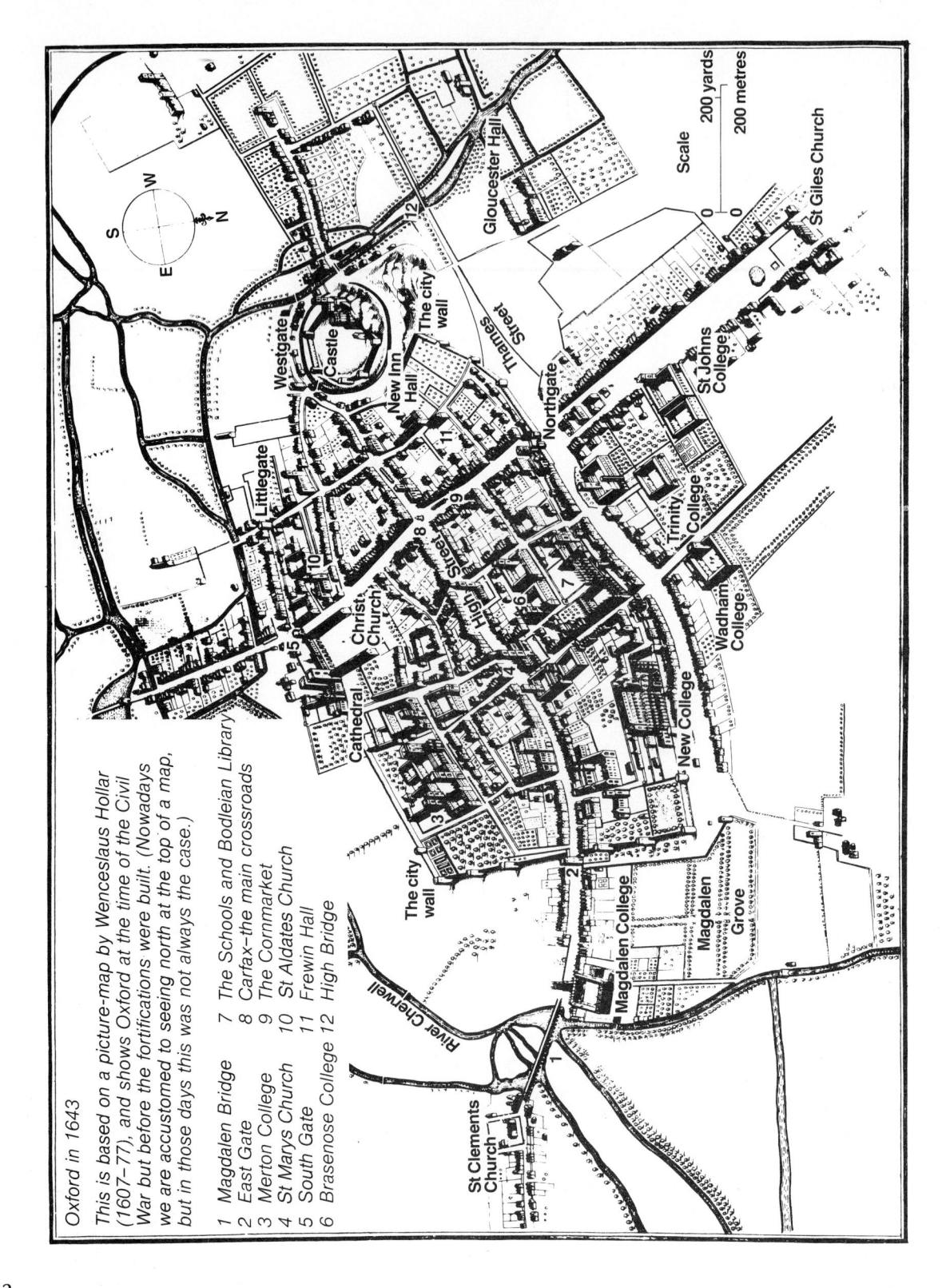

This is based on a picture-map by Wenceslaus Hollar (1607–77), and shows Oxford at the time of the Civil War but before the fortifications were built. (Nowadays we are accustomed to seeing north at the top of a map, but in those days this was not always the case.)

1. Magdalen Bridge
2. East Gate
3. Merton College
4. St Marys Church
5. South Gate
6. Brasenose College
7. The Schools and Bodleian Library
8. Carfax–the main crossroads
9. The Cornmarket
10. St Aldates Church
11. Frewin Hall
12. High Bridge

Money and supplies

The King was always short of money, and so it was not long before he ordered the Royal Mint to come from Shrewsbury to Oxford and to be set up at New Inn Hall. Colleges and townspeople were ordered to hand over their plate to be melted down and made into coins. About 900 kg of silver and gold were collected. St Johns College tried to avoid handing over its plate by offering the King £800 in place of it, but the King just thanked the College for the money and took the plate as well!

On the other hand, one of the Fellows of Brasenose College was so cross at seeing the *kan* which he had himself presented to his college being removed, that he 'saved' it (i.e. removed it secretly from the pile). Anthony Wood was not so lucky. He reports that the plate which had been given to him:

tankard

> at his christening by his godfathers and godmother — which was considerable — was carried by his majesty's command to the mint at New Inn, and there turned into money to pay for his majesty's armies.

This is the beautiful 'Oxford Crown Piece' which was produced at New Inn Hall. There were four crowns in a £1 so it was a valuable coin. Notice the fine detail in the tiny city of Oxford (OXON) under the horse's belly, and see how the artist has given a feeling of movement to the design by the way he has depicted the horse's mane and tail, and the King's sash and hair.

1 Can you match up the Latin words of the inscriptions with the English meanings given below? (Note that some of the words are abbreviated, and that where there should be a U the artist has used a V.)

'Heads' side: Charles, by the grace of God, King of Great Britain, France and Ireland.

'Tails' side: *around rim*: May God arise and his enemies be scattered

                across middle: The Protestant Religion, the Laws of England, and a Free Parliament.

2 Which, if any, of these inscriptions might have been used just as well by the Roundheads on a coin of their own?

Compare the 'heads' side of this coin and that of a modern 10p piece and write down any features they have in common.

In spite of this newly minted coinage, the King was soon in desperate need of money again. He 'borrowed' £2000 from the university and £2000 from the city and also asked the citizens to contribute £200 a week towards the cost of the fortifications. In addition Oxfordshire and the university were required during the winter of 1642–3 to pay for the upkeep of six regiments of cavalry (about 2250 men) at a cost of £1176 a week. But it was not only money that the ordinary people had to provide; they also often found their goods and livestock being taken over for use by the garrison. Cattle, horses, corn – none were safe from the military. On one occasion, Wood tells us, 'a drove of fat great oxen, being brought out of Buckinghamshire, were driven into Christ Church quadrangle early in the morning'. Unfortunately it turned out that these beasts belonged to the Earl of Caernarvon, a supporter of the King, and so most of them had to be given back to him! However, all was well because 'upon the Wednesday or Thursday after there came to Oxford another drove of oxen and about 300 sheep, which were true pillages from his majesty's enemies'.

The war of words

The King soon realised that words can be weapons as well as swords; and he was fortunate in finding, in John Birkenhead, a witty writer to produce a weekly newsletter for the Royalist cause. It was entitled *Mercurius Aulicus, communicating the Intelligence and affairs of the Court to the rest of the Kingdom.* It cost a penny in Oxford where it was printed, but copies were smuggled to London – mostly by women, apparently, who disguised themselves as beggars and picked up and passed on copies which had been secretly left in agreed places along the way. In London the paper was reprinted and sold for as much as 18 pence a copy. It does not sound as if Birkenhead was particularly attractive: someone of the time said that:

> he was exceedingly bold, confident, witty, not very grateful to his benefactors; would lie damnably. He was of middling stature, great goggly eyes, not of sweet aspect.

However, he was very quick not only to record the Royalists' doings in the most favourable light, but to make fun of the enemy as well. For example, when a Parliament news-sheet announced incorrectly that the Royalist Sir Jacob Astley, a one-time Governor of Oxford, had been killed, Birkenhead commented:

> Sir Jacob Astley lately slain at Gloucester desires to know, was he slain with a musket or a cannon bullet?

Aulicus's scathing entry for 1 September 1644 reads:

cocked

> no less than 150 rebels came from Banbury to Wolvercote, where some of them with their pistols *spanned* rushed into the church, while the preacher was in the pulpit.

He then describes how two gentlemen and a few others:

> forced the rebels to quit the church; made the door good against those without, and then disarmed as many as were within. One gentleman with no other weapons but a pair of white gloves, mastered two rebels at once, till they begged for *quarter* on their knees (the first time they ever kneeled in a church). At last the rebels fled from the church.

quarter — mercy

1 How does the writer make it seem that only a few Cavaliers drove off the Roundheads?

2 Why does the Royalist say this was the 'first time they ever kneeled in a church'? (Look back at page 3.)

3 Parliament eventually hit back at Aulicus with their own news-sheet *Mercurius Britanicus*. Imagine you are its author, and write an account from Parliament's point of view, either of the Wolvercote raid or of the incident involving the 'drove of oxen' (see page 24).

Another vigorous Royalist writer was John Taylor, nicknamed the Water Poet. Of humble origins, he had been press-ganged into the navy for a while before becoming a Thames waterman. He usually wrote in verse, and became almost hysterical in his loyalty when in 1642 he made his way to Oxford to see the King:

> In Christ Church garden, then a gladsome sight was
> My Sovereign Lord and many a Peer and Knight was, . . .
> His gracious eye did see where I did stand straight,
> He came to me, puts forth his Royal hand straight,
> Which on my knees, I humbly kneeled and kissed it,
> I rather had left all I had than missed it.

His loyalty extended to other members of the royal family as well. Read what he had to say to a Roundhead critic who had called the King's nephew 'Rupert' and not 'Prince Rupert'. He wrote: 'Prince Rupert whom your sauciness is pleased to call plain Rupert, as if his Highness and your Knaveship were all fellows at football . . .'

Portrait of John Taylor, the Water Poet, by an unknown artist

But Taylor had no money and had to find a job in Oxford:

> To some employment I myself must settle,
> Fire must be had to boil the pot and kettle.
> Then by the Lords Commissioners and also
> By my good King (whom all true subjects call so)
> I was commanded by the Water Bailey
> To see the rivers cleansed both nights and daily.
> Dead hogs, dogs, cats and well flayed carrion horses
> Their noisome corpses soiled the waters' courses;
> Both swines' and stable dung, beasts' guts and garbage,
> Street dirt, with gardeners' weeds and rotten herbage.

rotting rubbish	And from those waters' filthy *putrefaction*,
	Our meat and drink were made, which bred infection.
hard work	Myself and partner, with cost, pains and *travail*
rotting meat	Saw all made clean, from *carrion*, mud and gravel.
	Besides at all commands, we served all warrants,
	To take boats for most necessary errands,
	To carry ammunition, food and fuel,
	(The last of which last winter was a jewel).

This verse gives us a vivid, if disgusting, picture of the state of the Thames and Cherwell. The population of Oxford was greatly swollen at this time by the arrival of the Court and the army, and the rivers obviously provided a considerable health hazard.

1 Besides acting as a sewer and a source from which 'our meat and drink were made', what other purpose does Taylor tell us the river was used for?

2 Which line tells us that fuel was in very short supply the previous winter?

3 It was unusual for a man like John Taylor to have his portrait painted, and it probably shows that he was quite well known. Compared to the portraits on page 5, what differences can you see that show he was not high-born?

The grandeur of Christ Church made it a suitable place for the King to live whenever he was in Oxford. Merton, where the Queen lived, was only a few minutes' walk away.

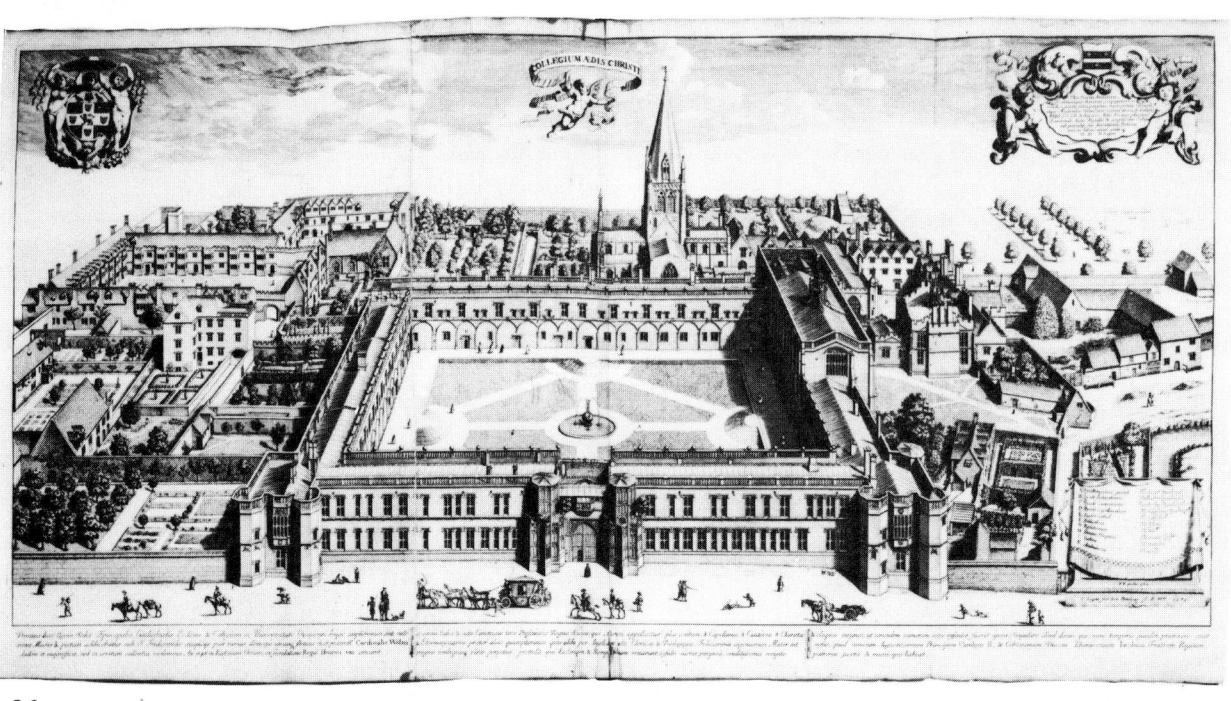

People at war

Charles I, by Le Sueur

The Court

The King established a regular routine during his stay at Christ Church, Oxford's largest college. An eye-witness writes:

> he would himself once or twice a week take horse and go about the town, to view both within and without the works, and be among his *ordinance* where they stood upon their carriages: he kept his hours most exactly, both for his exercises and for his *dispatches*, as also his hours for admitting all sorts to come and speak with him. You might know where he would be at any hour from his rising, which was very early, to his walk he took in the garden, and so to Chapel and dinner; so after dinner if he *went not abroad*, he had his hours for writing and *discoursing*, or chess playing, or tennis.

guns

letters

did not go out
talking

Charles's French queen, Henrietta Maria, was a firm Catholic who was always urging the King to stronger action. Charles was devoted to her, and it was a great joy to him when in July 1643 she arrived to take up her lodgings in nearby Merton College. She had had an adventurous journey from the Yorkshire coast where her ship had landed after its voyage from the Netherlands. The house where she had slept the first night was bombarded by Parliament ships, and she was persuaded to seek safety in a ditch; but she was so unafraid of the shelling that she went back to the house to fetch her lapdog which her ladies had left behind.

Problems continued. The Parliament general, Fairfax, and his army were between her and Oxford, and it took nearly five months before she was reunited with her husband. Her arrival was doubly welcome to Charles because she brought with her 2000 foot soldiers, 1000 horses, a number of cannon and some well-filled supply wagons.

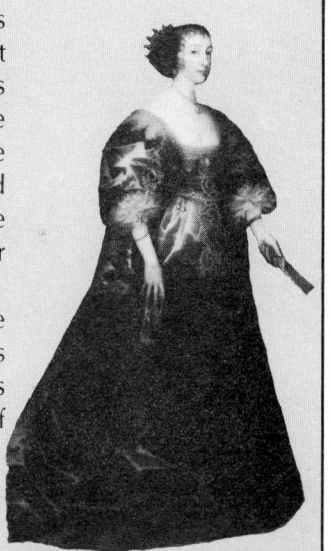

Queen Henrietta Maria, by an unknown artist, about 1636

A room used by Queen Henrietta Maria in Merton College

Charles, Prince of Wales, aged about 12, painted by the Court painter at Oxford, William Dobson, around the time of Edgehill.

The Queen enjoyed the civilised company at Oxford. A private way had been constructed between Christ Church and Merton so that she and Charles could come and go easily. The Queen enjoyed receiving company in her rooms and walking in the garden with her spaniels. There were musical entertainments and plays to amuse her (the King had appointed a Master of the Revels), new fashions to observe, love affairs to gossip about, weddings to attend – and funerals. But within a year, in April 1644 she left; she was pregnant, and had become unwell and depressed by the thought of being trapped in Oxford, and by all the talk she heard about the war. 'I am weary' she said, 'not of being beaten but of having heard it spoken of.' Charles and her two sons rode with her as far as Abingdon. When they parted the Queen fell into a faint from which she did not recover for thirty miles. The King never saw her again.

However, he did have other members of his family around him: the two young princes, for example, and his nephew Rupert, the great cavalry leader, with whom the King played tennis. The atmosphere was not all warlike; there was time for sport and merriment, and the King on more than one occasion went hunting at Woodstock. Prince Charles, the future Charles II, kept himself fit by attending Mr. William Stokes's dancing, vaulting and fencing school just outside the North Gate, where perhaps he learnt to perform the remarkable 'pass' illustrated below from Stokes' handbook.

There were small domestic problems too: for example, the King once had to send to his palace of Whitehall in London for some stockings and other small items. The House of Commons actually spent time debating whether a servant should be allowed to take them to Oxford. The motion was passed by 26 votes to 18, though Charles was not pleased to learn that such a matter was being debated at all!

The Pomado at the hind legg

A Council of War

Prince Rupert (on the left) with two of his fellow officers, by William Dobson

The one in the centre is dipping the cockade of his hat into his wine before he drinks a loyal toast to the King. The dog on the left probably belonged to Rupert, but is not the famous 'Boy'.

In spite of some pleasant times, the Court at Oxford was not a happy place, and the pressures of war created a great deal of tension and rivalry. There was the constant feeling of danger; regiments marching off to war; sadness when friends were killed or wounded. Many of the older courtiers resented the influence of Rupert and his forceful and often rash Cavaliers; and while she was there the Queen always argued for strong action. When the King summoned his Council of War these difficulties and disagreements often flared up. We know that a meeting of the Council took place in October 1643, and that the following people were present:

Members of the Council
Prince Rupert Aged 23. Nephew of the King. In spite of his youth, one of the few with real war experience on the Continent. A fearless commander of the cavalry. By 1643, he had already earned a great reputation: he and his poodle, 'Boy', who always went into battle with him, were much feared by Roundhead troops. He was quick-thinking, could be scornful and sarcastic to colleagues, and was prepared to shout anyone down.

Earl of Forth Aged 70. Lord Lieutenant General (i.e. commanding officer of the whole army under the King) until Rupert was appointed in his place in 1644. Rather deaf, so could conveniently not hear quarrels! A great reputation as a soldier.

Lord Percy General of the Ordnance (artillery). Bitter enemy of Rupert, who had blamed him for failing to get supplies from Oxford to Newport Pagnell (see page 31).

Sir Arthur Aston Aged 53. Governor of Oxford for a time. An ill-tempered, forceful soldier, a strict disciplinarian, and a Catholic. He was so unpopular among the garrison that when he was on his rounds in the city, he had to be protected 'by a guard consisting of four men in long red coats and halberds [a type of long-handled axe]'.

The Duke of Richmond Aged 31. Loyal personal friend and favourite cousin of the King; he would often smooth out Rupert's difficulties with courtiers.

Right: The Duke of Richmond, by Van Dyck, (1612-55)

Lord Byron The forceful Sir John Byron who made a flying visit to Oxford just before Edgehill (page 5). Created Baron Byron in October 1643 after the Battle of Newbury (see page 31).

General Legge Aged 36. Irish. A great friend of Rupert, and second in command to him in his cavalry regiment. Became Master of the Armoury, and set up the sword factory at Wolvercote. Had been a prisoner of Parliament but escaped in 1642.

Edward Hyde A methodical, rather fussy lawyer, always full of good advice. He had disliked the King's policies before the war, but was now a loyal and business-like Royalist. When he heard of the death of his close friend, Lord Falkland, at the Battle of Newbury, he called the war 'odious and detestable'.

The King Aged 43. Not good at deciding firmly on a course of action. When his advisers disagreed, he would withdraw into dignified silence, and seldom tried to settle matters.

Edward Hyde, later Earl of Clarendon, (1609-74)

The military situation by 1643

Although the King failed to take London in 1642, the situation now looked more hopeful. He planned a three-pronged advance on London: he would attack from Oxford, the Earl of Newcastle from the north, and Sir Ralph Hopton from the south-west. Royalist victory seemed to be in sight. But the plan failed. The important Parliament towns of Hull and Plymouth could not be taken, and the troops of Newcastle and Hopton would not march off to London leaving their rear unprotected and their homes at risk. Although Rupert captured Bristol, the King was unable to take Gloucester, and so it was not safe for him to advance on London, with a hostile town behind him and no help from the other two generals.

These recent events would have affected the Council's discussions:

4 September 1643 Exeter taken by Royalists.

20 September 1643 Battle of Newbury. At this battle Charles and Rupert, assisted by Prince Maurice and the Duke of Richmond, intercepted the Earl of Essex on his way back to London from Gloucester. The Royalists, who were badly lacking in ammunition, suffered terrible casualties including the death of two earls and the Secretary of State, Lord Falkland. The battle was indecisive. Essex was able to go on to London, and Charles returned to Oxford. Both were greeted on their homecoming with enthusiasm by their supporters, as though they had won a victory.

6 October 1643 Royalists seized Newport Pagnell to cut London's supply line from the Midlands (see map, page 19); but they had to surrender on 27 October because ammunition did not reach them from Oxford.

11 October 1643 Further north, at Winceby in Leicestershire, Cromwell's newly trained cavalry beat a Royalist force. 800 prisoners and 26 flags were taken. This was the quickest and easiest victory achieved by either side up to that time.

1 On a copy of the map on page 13 draw in arrows to show the King's three-pronged plan of attack. Use this map and the one on page 19 as you work out the next questions.

2 Using the account of the military situation and the time chart on pages 48 and 49, make a list in two columns of Royalist *Successes* and *Failures* by October 1643.

3 Imagine you are present at this Council of War. Rupert might well urge an advance on London because his cavalry is still fairly intact despite the Battle of Newbury, and Newport Pagnell could perhaps be won back. Cromwell is some distance away, but the success achieved by his new cavalry is worrying, so others might argue more cautiously. Write down in dialogue form, like a play, the conversation that might take place.

Lord Falkland, Secretary of State to the King in Oxford, after Van Dyck, painted before the war.

His friend, Edward Hyde, called him 'that incomparable young man'. Falkland probably committed suicide during the battle of Newbury by riding ahead of his troops, straight into the ranks of the enemy.

Strangers and citizens

Crowded houses

Many newcomers now crowded into Oxford around Charles and his family: courtiers, high-ranking officers, Royalist Members of Parliament, noblemen and their ladies, the artist William Dobson, and many other royal servants, including the King's surgeon, his apothecary, and his sewing woman, as well as poulterers, bakers, candle-makers and coal-carriers. Some ordinary soldiers were put in camps or churches, but a great many were in the city too, including the King's Lifeguards in their red coats. Seventeenth-century armies were also accompanied by women – both wives and less respectable characters – who often acted as nurses and cooks. Room had to be found for all these 'strangers' in colleges and private houses. The houses must have been full to overflowing. Although some of them had only one room upstairs and one down, they were often forced to hold several soldiers and conditions would have been very cramped.

Three houses in St Aldates

This photograph, probably taken about forty years ago, shows the houses (described on the opposite page) with additions made after 1644, including an extra storey. 31 and 32 were originally two small houses; by 1644 they had been made into one.

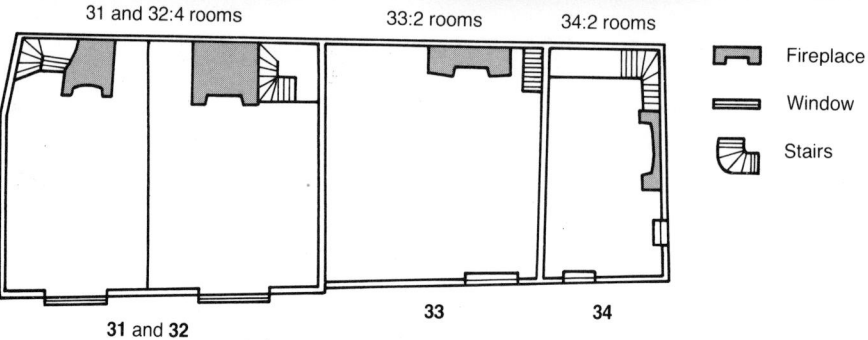

Probable layout of the three two-storey houses in 1644, showing the first floor. The ground floor would have been similar.

The Royalists took several censuses in Oxford, counting town dwellers and the strangers who were billeted on them. They needed the information for different reasons: to calculate provisions; to ensure that everyone helped with the fortifications, and to impose fines if they did not; and, in January 1644, to see how much room could be made for the Members of Parliament whom the King had just summoned. One list, made by the royal official Edward Heath, still survives. It deals with 74 houses in the area of St Aldates. This is a busy area today, and it was crowded then too; 408 'strangers' were living in those 74 quite small houses, in addition to the people who normally lived there. These are the occupants listed by Heath in three houses, whose approximate size we know.

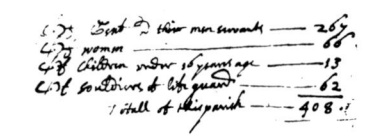

A facsimile of part of the 'Exact Accompt' (census) made by Edward Heath, relating to the St Aldates area

	31 and 32	33	34
HOUSEHOLDER	Mistress Jane Hawkes, widow	John Massey	Mistress Elizabeth Treadwell, widow
FAMILY	Stepson and wife, who may not have lived there. Her husband John Hawkes, a prosperous butcher, died in 1642.	Unknown (but this does not necessarily mean he had no family — they are not entered on the census).	Her husband John had been a cordwainer (leather worker), and probably died in 1642. She probably had a son, Matthew, a brewer, but it is not known if he lived there.
OCCUPATION	She still carried on her husband's business as a butcher.	Parchment-maker.	—
STRANGERS	Colonel David Scrymgeour, an important Scots officer who had come south with the Earl of Forth, and fought with Prince Rupert. He had three men with him — soldiers or servants. Sergeant Major Lugwood, probably in the same Scots regiment, and one man. TOTAL: SIX STRANGERS	A corporal of the Life Guards. It is also known that two soldiers died at this house in 1644 and 1645, so John Massey may have looked after wounded or sick soldiers at different times. These two deaths took place when plague was raging in Oxford.	One sergeant and two soldiers of the Life Guards.

FACTS WE DO NOT KNOW: The above information should help us to guess what life was like for the people in these houses, but we do not know how eating, sleeping and living arrangements worked, nor how they all got on with each other. The householders were probably not paid for lodging strangers.

How much has this greedy soldier collected from local inhabitants?

Law and order

Such overcrowding, and the presence of large numbers of soldiers, led to drunken quarrels and riots. The soldiers and courtiers quarrelled among themselves too: 'Sir Arthur Aston wounded in the side in the dark by a scuffle in the street', for example; and 'two gentlemen fell out and fought for a horse that was given between them, and one of them run the horse through and . . . Prince Rupert came forth with a pole-axe and parted them.'

The townspeople were accustomed to the sight of men being hanged, because quite early in the war a gallows had been set up at Carfax. There was also a punishment 'horse' for less serious crimes; Anthony Wood gives as examples, 'being a turn coat from the King to the Parliament and backward again, and for selling arms etc.' It was made of two planks, nailed together to make an uncomfortable ridge. The offender had to ride on the 'horse' with a musket tied to his legs. (You could make a sketch of the punishment horse in use.)

Prisoners of war were occasionally kept in churches (1100 of them, briefly, after the capture of Cirencester); but the majority were locked up in the Castle. Conditions there were very bad, with no fires or bedding, and sometimes so little water that they had to scoop up the puddles in the rough exercise yards if they wanted a drink. No wonder that many preferred to join the Royalist army, rather than remain there.

Disease

With perhaps five or six thousand troops in the town, and bad conditions, disease was bound to be a problem. (Remember also what John Taylor had to say about the unhealthy state of the rivers.) In 1643 there was an outbreak of 'camp fever' (probably typhus); according to a Roundhead spy, 40 people a week died including the Governor of Oxford, Sir William Pennyman. It was caused, so a local doctor said, by the presence of the army whose 'filth and nastiness of diet, worse lodging, unshifted apparel [unchanged clothes]', were bound to cause disease. So it is not surprising that in 1644 and 1645 another killer disease attacked Oxford. The people called it 'the plague' but it does not seem to have been bubonic plague. Still, some people may have put their faith in the remedies for plague which John Taylor mentions:

> bunch of fragrant flowers
> a drug to fight off germs

One with a piece of tasselled well-tarred rope
Doth with that *nosegay* keep himself in hope:
Another doth a wisp of *wormwood* pull
And with great judgement crams his nostrils full:
A third takes off his socks from his sweating feet
And makes them his perfume along the street!

The City Council were certainly so worried about 'the great danger of breeding an infection amongst us', because of the filth in the streets, that the wages of the 'scavengers [refuse collectors]' were doubled.

Fire

Fire was always a danger in seventeenth-century towns, so it was not surprising that there was a serious one in wartime Oxford in 1644. Because of the overcrowding, people often had to do their cooking in rooms not equipped for fire-making. Anthony Wood tells us:

> On Sunday 8 October happened a dreadful fire in Oxon... It began about two of the clock in the afternoon in a little poor house on the south side of Thames Street occasioned by a foot-soldier's roasting a pig which he had stolen. The wind being very high and in the north, blew the flames southward very quick and strongly, and burnt all houses and stables that extend from the North gate.

If you look at the map on page 22 you will be able to see how much of the city was damaged. The boundaries of the fire were approximately:
on the east: the street joining North Gate and South Gate
on the west: the street running from New Inn Hall to Littlegate
on the south: the street leading from South Gate to Littlegate
on the north: the city wall.

This Dutch picture of 1652 gives us a good idea of the danger and panic created by a fire in a crowded city.

Some of the buildings were of stone and escaped serious damage, but most were of timber; and the ten bakehouses and eight brewhouses which went up in flames contained stores of highly inflammable material. Between 200 and 300 houses were destroyed. Among them were two owned by Anthony Wood's mother. As a result, she could no longer afford to keep Anthony at his school at Thame, and he had to return to Oxford.

The fire raged for 10–11 hours, and could easily be seen by the forces of Parliament in Abingdon. People in Oxford feared that these enemy forces would take advantage of the confusion caused by the fire, and make an attack on the city. Although this did not happen, the Parliament newspapers in London were quick to make comments. One of them pointed out that as the fire took place on a Sunday, it was obviously a judgement by God on 'that seat of wickedness' (ie Oxford) for 'breaking the Sabbath'.

Demands on the city

The old bad feeling between the city and the university still remained, and now the City Council was also irritated by Royalist demands for money and co-operation. For example, a city regiment had to be provided to defend the town, and the citizens had to pay and train the soldiers. All sorts of arguments were found to avoid this; and finally the King himself had to write to the mayor in strong terms, commanding him 'that without further delay you fully raise the said regiment and arm the same, or *certify us in whose default* it is that you do not perform the same.'

let us know whose fault

Over a year later the regiment was still not properly organised or paid. The City Council refused to co-operate with the Royalist officer put in command, and said that he was only aiming:

> at his own ends and to enrich himself by the city, and not taking into his consideration the poverty which this city is fallen into.... Besides he hath *affronted* the late mayor by assaulting him in his place and seat in the city office, a thing not to be forgotten by this house!

insulted

Three aldermen were even imprisoned by the King for a time, and when they were released they were compensated for what 'they had suffered for the city'.

There were obviously a great many problems for the townspeople of Oxford because their city had become the Royalist capital, especially as many of them sympathised with Parliament. However there were advantages too – above all, the money that could be made from supplying the needs of the courtiers and soldiers. For most people, the day-to-day business of earning a living was always more important than anything else. So they saw no point in being too uncooperative or rebellious.

1 Make a list of reasons why the city was so uncooperative over providing a regiment for the King.

2 What other grievances might ordinary citizens have had against the Royalist garrison?

3 Begin a journal written by an ordinary Oxford citizen, which starts in the autumn of 1642. Decide what trade you follow, and whether you are male or female. The information on houses in St Aldates on page 33 will be useful. Bring in some of the main events and problems – use the time chart of events at the end of the book to help you, and take the story to the end of 1644 for the moment. You will be able to finish it when you have reached the end of the book.

You could be involved in: building fortifications;
cleaning streets or rivers;
serving the Court at Christ Church;
billeting soldiers;
disease;
the fire.

Anne would probably have worn a fashionable costume like this when she first arrived in Oxford; later, as a married woman living in a wartime city, she probably dressed more soberly like the lady below.

By the sword divided

One visitor to Oxford at this time was Ann, Lady Fanshawe. In her memoirs she wrote:

> My father commanded my sister and myself to come to him to Oxford, where the Court then was; but we, that had till that hour lived in great plenty and great order, found ourselves like fishes out of water.

She goes on to say that they were forced to live in a baker's house where they had only one proper meal a day, badly cooked at that; and they were short of money and clothing. They were depressed by the continual talk of 'losing and gaining of towns and men'; and also by the sight from the windows of 'the sad spectacle of war, sometimes plague, sometimes sickness of other kinds by reason of so many people being packed together'.

No wonder Ann wanted to leave. She had arrived in Oxford in 1643, aged 18; had married Sir Richard Fanshawe the next year; and in 1645 had to see her husband go off to Bristol with the staff of the Prince of Wales. In her memoirs she describes her husband leaving her just after the birth of her first son, and how although he was a reserved man 'he was extremely afflicted to tears' because 'it was the first time we had

37

parted a day since we married', and he was 'leaving me with a dying child, which did die 2 days later, in a garrison town, extreme weak, and very poor'.

Two months later her husband managed to send her fifty pieces of gold to pay her expenses to join him. Happy at the thought of seeing him soon, and excited by the sound of drums in the street, she went up on a mound in St Johns College garden; there she leaned against a tree to see the soldiers march past. The commander of the troops, a friend of the family, seeing her there, 'in compliment gave us a volley of shot, and one of their muskets being loaded shot a brace of bullets not two inches above my head as I leaned to the tree.' Soon after this narrow escape she was reunited with her husband, and in course of time had 14 children.

Sir Richard Fanshawe, Anne's husband, by William Dobson

1 From what Ann Fanshawe says about wartime Oxford, what do you think her life was like before the war?

2 Write a short character sketch of Ann, saying how you think she coped with her wartime life.

Of course Ann was not the only person whose life was 'by the sword divided'; and at least in her case there was no problem of split loyalties within the family, as there was with the Roundhead supporters John Smyth and Walter Cave (see page 11) both of whom had pro-Royalist brothers. Though John Smyth had been Mayor in 1639 and MP for Oxford in 1640, the Court disapproved of him so strongly that he thought it better to leave Oxford and go to Abingdon.

Perhaps Lucy Heath's story is one of the saddest. Her husband Edward, a strong Royalist, was devoted to her; but he was very busy because he was appointed to help supervise the work on the city fortifications, and to assist in drawing up lists of people to do the work. He also organised the census described on page 33, so Lucy had to cope with all the family problems. For safety's sake, their three children had been left in houses owned by the Heath family near Oakham in modern Leicestershire. Lucy had married Edward when she was only 13; and had borne her first child (who did not survive), before she was 15. Two more babies died soon afterwards; and then Margaret was born, the only one of Lucy's nine children to survive beyond the age of six. Even in those days when so many young children died, Lucy was particularly unlucky.

Her life was not made any easier by the fact that her cousin, Unton Croke, a leading Oxford citizen, was a Parliament supporter; it seems that, like John Smyth, he thought it wiser to leave a town as Royalist as Oxford, and go to live in his other house a few miles away at Marston. To make matters worse, one of Unton's sons was a Roundhead captain of

Horse (cavalry). Also one of Heath's houses near Oakham, where Margaret was supposed to be safe, was raided by some Roundhead troops from nearby Rockingham Castle, who plundered it of money, bedding, corn and halberds. Lucy had to write to the MP for that area, a strong Parliamentarian, to beg him to allow Margaret a safe passage to Oxford. It seems that permission was granted, because Margaret in due course joined her parents.

Three months later the Heaths heard of the death of their son, Robert, who was not quite two, at the other 'safe' house. Lucy's desperation and grief can be glimpsed in the letter she now wrote to a friend near Oakham:

> I know you cannot but hear of the *rigour* is used against me and my husband in the *sequestrating* of all the estate, not leaving anything for me and my innocent children but denying so much as might bury my dear babe I have now newly lost; and to this is added this time when I most need them, being big with child, the taking away of all my linen even to my very baby *clouts* and mantles, all which I confess I much more prize *in regard* they were the gift of my dear mother.

hard treatment
confiscating

clothes
because

■ What were the three things which were upsetting Lucy when she wrote this letter?

The child she was expecting was born at Oxford six months later, and died within six weeks. Lucy herself did not survive much longer, for within half a year she too was dead, at the age of only 27. She was worn out by so many pregnancies, and the anguish of a woman caught in the conflicts of a civil war.

■ Lucy's daughter, Margaret, was about 8 when she arrived in Oxford, and had probably been separated from her parents for two years. Describe her feelings and impressions when she arrives in Oxford and sees her parents again.

Baby clothes in well-to-do families were beautifully sewn by hand, and were a treasured possession, passed down from mother to daughter.

Detail from 'The Family of Arthur, Lord Capel' painted by Cornelius Johnson in about 1639

These two sons of Lord Capel were painted in about 1639. The younger son is probably about two, and like all upper class toddlers in the seventeenth century he wears long skirts. His seven-year-old brother is old enough to be dressed as a miniature adult.

39

Roundhead victory

The three banners of different parliamentary regiments shown on these two pages used slogans and pictures to inspire the soldiers.

Parliament closes in

From early in 1644 the Royalist fortunes began to slip. The Scots joined Parliament, and the King's Irish troops proved unsatisfactory. Although Rupert won a brilliant victory at Newark in March 1644, he was completely outmatched at Marston Moor near York in July by Cromwell's 'Ironsides' – the nickname given to the new Roundhead cavalry force. Rupert's dog, 'Boy', which had always seemed to bring him luck, was killed.

A battle in Yorkshire must have seemed very far away to the people of Oxford. They would have been much more worried about an attempt by the two Parliament generals, the Earl of Essex and Sir William Waller, to trap the King in Oxford. Essex crossed the Thames at Sandford and marched through Cowley and Bullingdon Green to Islip. From there he went on to Woodstock. Mercurius Aulicus managed to make scornful fun out of this event, which was in fact a useful Roundhead reconnaissance. He wrote:

rash
fortifications

guns

> The rebels marched within two miles of the town, with drum and colours towards Islip some of them being so *wanton* as to leave the body, and come in parties towards the *works*, perhaps that they might say to their friends in London that they had seen Oxford for their money. But whilst they were in this bravado, a shot was made by Sir John Heydon from one of the great *ordinance* on St Clements bulwarks which fell so happily amongst them that it killed a trooper and hurt one of their horses, and put them into such a fright that they all ran presently towards their body in great confusion and amazement. And yet this is reported to their friends in London for a gallant action.

The King watched a scouting party of enemy cavalry from the top of Magdalen tower, and there was some talk of surrender. 'What', he said, 'I may be found in the hands of the Earl of Essex, but I shall be dead first!'

Waller had crossed the Thames at Newbridge and marched towards Eynsham, but the King showed his lack of fear by taking time off for a day's hunting at Woodstock, and then returned to Oxford. He tricked Waller into thinking he was going to attack Abingdon, and slipped away northwards in the evening with 3000 horse and 2500 foot, through Wolvercote, Witney and Burford, and on to Worcester. Lighted matchcord (normally used for lighting muskets) was left in the hedges around Islip, to trick Essex into believing the King's army was still there.

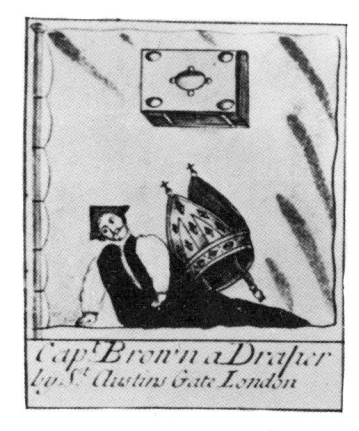

The Bible conquers a bishop and his mitre

- On a copy of the map on page 19 trace the routes taken by Essex, Waller and the King.

The King returned to Oxford four months later, pleased that he had defeated Essex at Lostwithiel in Cornwall. He reviewed his army of 1500 men on Bullingdon Green and appointed Rupert Lieutenant General. Two Parliament commissioners now visited him at Oxford with peace proposals, but Charles rejected them scornfully. After wintering in Oxford, he moved off again in May 1645.

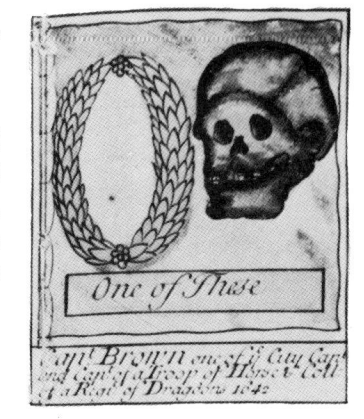

This regiment is prepared for either death or glory

The noose tightens

Within a week or two there was a new threat to the city – the Parliament commander-in-chief, Sir Thomas Fairfax, had joined Cromwell on the outskirts of the town, and Oxford was besieged.

The attackers threw up earthworks east of the Cherwell, threatening Magdalen bridge; and crossed the Cherwell itself at Marston with four regiments of foot and 13 carriages, to threaten the northern approach to Oxford. The Royalists, in reply, flooded the meadows and burned outlying houses to deprive the enemy of cover. Gaunt House fell to the Roundheads, but the Oxford garrison made a successful raid on the Parliament guard on Headington Hill.

However, Fairfax was obviously uneasy about keeping up the siege while the King was on the loose elsewhere, as we can see from this letter that he wrote to his father:

> I am very sorry we should spend our time unprofitably before a town while the King hath power to strengthen himself. The Parliament is *sensible* of this now aware and therefore hath sent me directions to raise the siege and march to Buckingham. It is the earnest desire of the Army to follow the King, but the endeavours of others to prevent it hath so much prevailed.

1 What does he mean by 'the King hath power to strengthen himself'?

2 '... endeavours of others to prevent it...' This phrase suggests that there was some opposition to raising the siege. Write down the reasons that might have been put forward for keeping it going.

So, a few days later, Fairfax abandoned the siege and headed for the Midlands. With Oliver Cromwell, he confronted the King on 14 June 1645 at Naseby near Leicester, in the most decisive battle of the Civil War. It

Sir Thomas Fairfax (1612–71)

was a complete disaster for Charles: he lost 1000 men dead and 5000 as prisoners or wounded. All his banners, artillery, arms, ammunition, baggage and wagons fell to the enemy, together with all the private papers in his own coach. Edward Hyde wrote: 'The King and the Kingdom were lost at Naseby.'

But Charles himself was not yet in the hands of the enemy; and by November he was back at Oxford, weary after 1200 miles of travel.

The final siege

Whilst the King had been absent 3000 cattle and sheep and 45 cartloads of provisions had been brought into the city because it was obvious that a new siege was likely to be started. This seemed all the more probable when the last sizeable Royalist force in the district was defeated on its way to join the King.

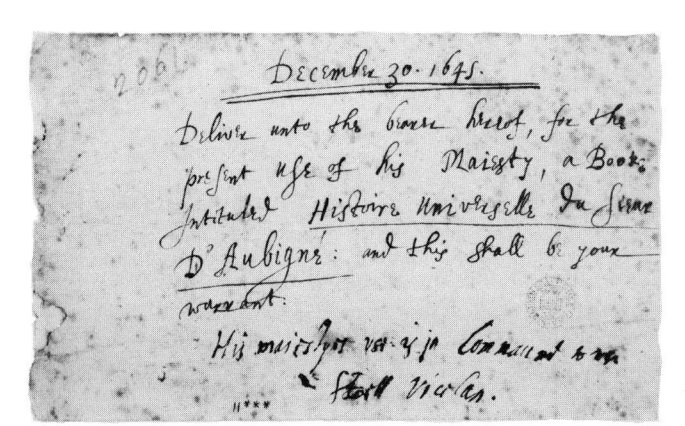

Charles decided to study other civil wars while he was in Oxford, and so sent this message to the Bodleian Library asking for a book on the subject to be delivered to him; but books in the Library's great collection are never lent out, so the Keeper of the Library refused the King's request!

By April 1646 Oxford was surrounded by Parliamentary forces. The King finally had to admit that there was no hope of victory. He preferred to surrender to the Scots rather than to Parliament, and fled from the besieged city in disguise. Wearing a servant's clothes and with his hair cut short, he and two companions rode secretly out over Magdalen bridge at 3 am; the Governor of Oxford sped them on their way with a cry to the King of 'Farewell, Harry!'

After Charles's departure the noose tightened further around Oxford. As soon as Parliament heard that the King had gone, they ordered Fairfax to let no one leave the city except to discuss surrender. The Roundhead headquarters were set up at Headington, and strong points were established on Headington Hill ('to receive and lodge 3000 men'), and also at Marston, Cowley and Elsfield. A bridge was built over the Cherwell at Marston, and a defensive line was constructed from

Headington Hill around St Clements, in some places so close to the city fortifications that the opposing soldiers could 'parley [speak] one with another' (see map, page 21). Inside the town itself the store of siege provisions was opened up, and the death penalty was ordered for soldiers found taking food from civilians.

The stage seemed set for a long siege. However, it soon became apparent that neither side really wanted one. On 11 May Fairfax sent in a trumpeter with a surrender note for the Governor of the city:

> Sir, I do by these, summon you to deliver up the City of Oxford into my hands, for the use of the Parliament. I very much desire the preservation of that place (so famous for learning) from ruin, which inevitably is like to fall upon it, except you *concur*. You may have honourable terms for yourself and all within that garrison if you reasonably accept thereof. I desire the answer this day, and remain, Your Servant, Tho: Fairfax.

agree

This was not immediately accepted, perhaps because it might have seemed dishonourable if the garrison had put up no resistance at all; and because there was some disagreement between the soldiers who wanted to fight it out, and the remaining Royalist Councillors who wished to surrender. So a limited exchange of artillery fire started. A cannon ball from Marston hit the side of the hall at Christ Church, and a shot from the Oxford defences killed a Roundhead colonel on Headington Hill.

■ From the map on page 21 work out the distance from Marston to Christ Church, and decide whether this was likely to have been a chance hit or the result of deliberate aim (see also page 20 for range of cannon).

About a hundred of the garrison tried their luck at restocking their food supplies, by dashing out on horseback in an attempt to seize some grazing cattle. They were driven back; but Fairfax, who perhaps was uncertain of the amount of food still available in Oxford, sent the Duke of York, the King's younger son, a present of 'bucks, lambs, veals, and capons'.

The garrison meanwhile had been in contact with the King, and they now received the royal permission to surrender. In his letter to the Governor, dated 18 May, he wrote:

> Trusty and well-beloved we greet you well. Being desirous to stop the further *effusion* of the blood of our subjects, and yet respecting the faithful services of all in that City of Oxford which have faithfully served us and hazarded their lives for us: we have thought it good to command you to quit that city, and disband the forces under your charge there, you receiving Honourable Conditions for you and them.

flowing

On 20 June, at Unton Croke's house at Marston, the Articles of Surrender were signed; and on 25 June the keys of the city were presented to

Fairfax. The King's hopes for 'honourable conditions' were granted. The garrison of about 3000 men were allowed to march out unharmed, and each soldier was issued with a pass of safe conduct home. Rupert and his brother received a safe conduct for ten days, after which they had to leave the country; the young Duke of York was conveyed to London for safe keeping.

The end of the story

For all Royalists there were difficult times ahead.

This picture of the execution of Charles I was published soon after the event. It clearly shows the scene in front of the Banqueting House in Whitehall, London, and the reactions both of the soldiers and the crowd.

Prince Rupert, by William Dobson, 1646

King Charles I was tried and publicly executed in January 1649 after many attempts at a settlement had failed, and more fighting had broken out. Such a thing had never happened to an English king before.

Queen Henrietta Maria bore their youngest child, Henrietta Anne, in Exeter late in 1644. Parliamentary forces were near, and she fled to France, leaving her baby in the care of friends. The King saw his child once while he was in the West Country, and called her 'my youngest and prettiest daughter'. After Parliament's victory, she was allowed to join her mother.

Prince Charles went into a long exile. After many difficulties he was finally restored as King Charles II in 1660.

The Duke of York managed to escape from his Parliamentary captors in London, and joined his brother in exile. He succeeded his brother in 1685 as the ill-fated King James II.

Prince Rupert lost the King's favour when he was forced to surrender Bristol in 1645 to a superior force. This portrait was painted in Oxford by

William Dobson just afterwards, and the background is unfinished because the siege was beginning, and Rupert had to leave. Compare this portrait to the one on page 29, and decide whether you think Rupert looks different after this shattering experience. He went into exile and took to the sea, organising naval attacks on Parliamentary shipping.

William Dobson   the artist went to London in 1646, and died in poverty the same year.

Edward Hyde   went into exile and was a loyal adviser to Charles II. In 1660 he was made the Earl of Clarendon and Lord Chancellor. Later he wrote a history of the times he had lived through, which has given historians a great deal of information.

Some **Royalists** went into exile. Others returned to their estates, many of which had suffered a good deal of damage during the war.

The University   had backed the losing side. There were few scholars in residence, and some dons and heads of colleges were expelled for a time. In 1649 Generals Fairfax and Cromwell paid an official visit to Oxford, and dined and played bowls in Magdalen College. Gradually life in the colleges returned to normal, but until Charles II was restored to his throne in 1660, the university lost its dominating position over the town.

For **the citizens of Oxford** life began to return to normal. Although there were still soldiers around, most of the citizens felt more friendly towards them, and there was no further danger of the war coming to the streets of the city.

Anthony Wood says he:

> found Oxford empty as to scholars, but pretty well *replenished* with Parliamentarian soldiers. Many of the inhabitants had gained great store of wealth from the Court and royalists that had for several years continued among them; but as for the young men of the city and university he [i.e. Wood] found many of them to have been *debauched* by bearing arms and doing the duties belonging to soldiers, as watching, warding, and sitting in *tippling-houses* for whole nights together.

Alderman Nixon's school, by Jessup

filled up

corrupted
inns

But there was no doubt what the City Council felt about the Royalist cause: only five days after the surrender they recalled the members who had been removed from office by the King's orders in 1642, and elected as Mayor their ringleader, Alderman John Nixon. Nixon became a very wealthy citizen and founded a school for boys in the city. Anthony Wood disliked him. He said he had such a 'smooth flattering tongue' and was so hard in his dealings that the scholars would say:

like alderman Nixon, hard and smooth like any *sleek-stone*

polishing stone

■ Wood says he did not care for Nixon because of his 'smooth flattering tongue'. Would he have any other reason to dislike him?

But even when a war is over, problems still exist.

In 1661 several inhabitants of Marston, the village on the outskirts of Oxford where Unton Croke had a house, complained about damage done to their land and property during the Civil War. They said that:

> in the time of the late wars and by reason of the Garrison of Oxford, their fields and lands did for the most part lie fresh and fallow and could not be manured and *husbanded* to any profit . . . and their houses were much ruined, decayed and wasted and their trees cut down and employed for the use of the said Garrison, and great part of their meadows were spoiled by digging of turfs for making the bulwarks in and about the said Garrison, and their cattle plundered and taken away.

farmed

1 What do you think is meant here by 'bulwarks'?

2 Who do you think plundered and took away their cattle, Royalists or Roundheads or both? Give reasons.

3 Do you think the villagers of Marston approved of their fields lying 'fresh and fallow'?

The city itself was saved from damage. The townspeople's houses were not harmed, and nor were the fine college buildings and churches. Fairfax also made sure that other features were preserved, as a writer of the time tells us:

> When Oxford was surrendered the first thing General Fairfax did was to set a good guard of soldiers to preserve the Bodleian Library. Tis said there was more hurt done by the cavaliers during the garrison by way of *embezzling* and cutting off chains of books, than there was since. He was a lover of learning and had he not taken this special care, that noble Library had been utterly destroyed.

stealing

1 How did General Fairfax safeguard the city of Oxford and all the people in it (soldiers and citizens)?

2 What is your impression of General Fairfax as a military commander?

3 Complete your journal written by an Oxford citizen (see page 37), finishing with the entry of Fairfax and his troops into the city.

War always brings sadness and suffering, and the people in Oxford during the Civil War, whether Royalist or Parliamentarian, had their full share. But at least there was no great loss of life as the siege ended, and a beautiful city was not destroyed. Many of the buildings which were there when the King's army filled the streets can still be seen today.

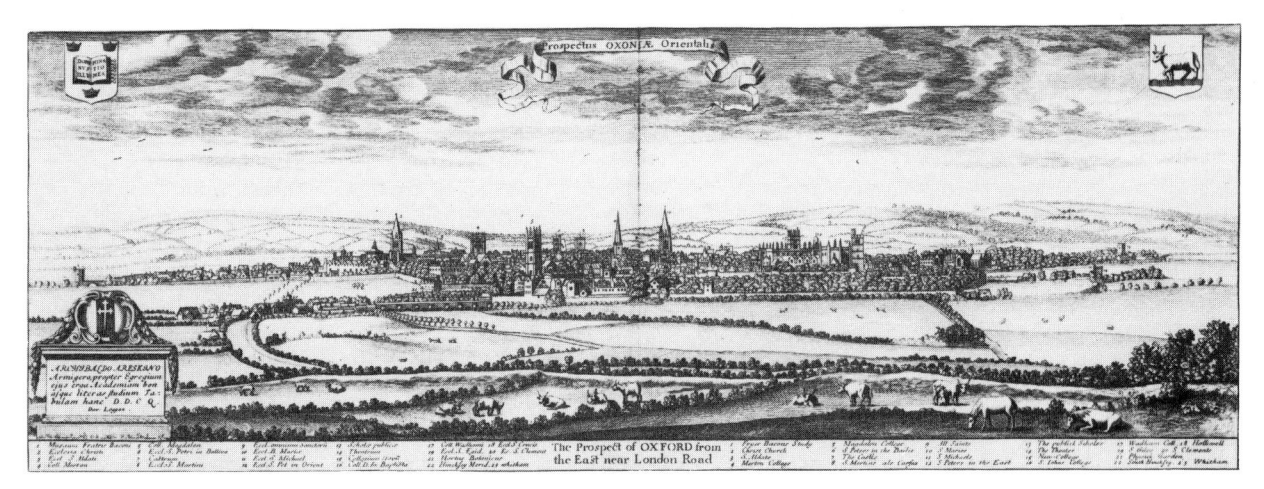

A view of Oxford a few years after the Civil War

A writer and his times

Anthony Wood (1632 – 95)

The writings of Anthony Wood are often quoted in this book, because they tell us a great deal about the times in which he lived. He was born in 1632 in a house opposite Merton College, and died in the same house sixty-three years later, after a lifetime spent almost entirely in Oxford. He said he remembered, as a small boy, seeing Charles I and his Queen riding into Christ Church, which must have been during their visit in 1635 (see page 8). He also remembered being kicked on the head by a carrier's horse while still very young, which left him with a 'slowness in apprehending the quickness of things'. Nevertheless, he remembered that the horse was called 'Mutton', and showed little sign later on of being slow-witted.

He started his education at New College School, but seems to have been sent away from Oxford to school in Thame for safety after the war started. He was only ten in 1642. When he was nineteen he became a scholar at Merton College, and spent the rest of his life in Oxford, writing books and notes about the history of the university and its great men, as well as his own diary. He used sixty volumes of notes left by a methodical and thorough don called Bryan Twyne, who had worked for Archbishop Laud in the 1630's and died in 1644. Anthony Wood was also very thorough, and took trouble to find things out for himself. He was a great gossip, and spent much time talking to people who knew about past times, especially the Civil War. He seems to have been disliked by many people: one person who knew him described him as not only 'a great blockhead, who has not one grain of good nature, good sense, good learning, but also a malicious scurrilous [unpleasantly rude] writer'. Obviously Anthony Wood upset him!

When you read Wood's writings, remember:

1. He was very young while the Civil War was going on.
2. He was not in Oxford for the later part of the war.
3. He could be very unpleasant about people, especially those who disagreed with him.
4. He was an enthusiastic Royalist, and devoted to his university, so he is bound to give that viewpoint.

But

5. He knew Oxford very well.
6. He knew a great many people who had been in Oxford during the war as adults, and found out a great deal from them.
7. He worked very hard to find out as much as he could, and often wrote about it in an interesting way.

Time chart of the Civil War

YEAR	MAIN EVENTS (mentioned either in *City at War* or *World of Change* core book)	EVENTS IN AND NEAR OXFORD
1642	**August** King's standard raised at Nottingham **October** BATTLE OF EDGEHILL **November** Royalists marched towards London Turnham Green	**August** Sir John Byron's visit to Oxford Lord Saye and Sele's visit to Oxford **October** The King's entry into Oxford, which became the Royalist capital Buildings began to be taken over by the garrison, and soldiers billeted on the citizens
1643	Royalist three-pronged attack on London planned **February** Royalists captured Cirencester **June** Battle of Chalgrove – John Hampden killed **July** Battle of Lansdowne near Bath Rupert captured Bristol **August** Royalist siege of Gloucester failed **September** First Battle of Newbury – Lord Falkland killed **October** Cromwell's Ironsides trained Royalists briefly held Newport Pagnell – Battle of Winceby Royalist siege of Hull failed **December** John Pym died	**February** 1100 prisoners brought in **March** Commissioners from Parliament arrived to discuss peace – no agreement **April** Fortifications round the city completed **June** The Mint set up **July** The Queen arrived **October** A meeting of the King's Council of War During 1643, an epidemic of 'camp fever' in the city
1644	Scots joined Parliament	Edward Heath's census of St Aldates The King summoned Parliament to Oxford **April** The Queen left Oxford for the West Country

YEAR	MAIN EVENTS (mentioned either in *City at War* or *World of Change* core book)	EVENTS IN AND NEAR OXFORD
1644	*June* Birth of Princess Henrietta at Exeter The Queen left for France *July* BATTLE OF MARSTON MOOR York and the North controlled by Parliament *September* Battle of Lostwithiel *October* Second Battle of Newbury	*June* Essex and Waller threatened Oxford Greenland House surrendered The King left Oxford for the West Country Battle of Cropredy Bridge *October* Fire in the city The King rejected peace proposals Epidemic of plague in the city during 1644
1645	New Model Army formed *May* Clubmen met at Bradbury, Dorset *June* BATTLE OF NASEBY 'The King and the Kingdom were lost at Naseby' *September* Prince Rupert surrendered Bristol	*April* Cromwell seized Bletchingdon House *May* The King left for the Midlands Godstow House and Gaunt House fell to Parliament First siege of Oxford by Fairfax began Fairfax left to pursue the King's army Epidemic of plague in the city during 1645
1646	*April* The King left Oxford for the last time Royalist surrender of Exeter	*April* Woodstock Manor fell to Parliament

The second siege of Oxford
May THE KING SURRENDERED TO THE SCOTS AT NEWARK
June SURRENDER OF OXFORD
Battle of Stow-on-the-Wold (the end of the first Civil War)

Charles I summoned a Royalist parliament in Oxford in January 1644 to make his government look more legal, though it had little effect on events. It met in Convocation House which is beyond the Divinity School in the Bodleian Library.

Find out more for yourself

Visits and local research. Wherever you live, you can almost certainly find out about events in the Civil War in your area, and your local library will help you.

If you live near Oxford you can visit some of the places mentioned below. If you live further away, you may be able to arrange a special visit, perhaps when you are on holiday.

Although Oxford is now a busy modern city, you can still find a great deal of what was there in the seventeenth century. If you climb the tower of the university church of St Marys in the High Street, and use the maps in this book, you can get a very good idea of the layout of the wartime city, and how small it was. You can also visit many of the colleges, most of which have changed little. Christ Church and Merton, where the court was based, and New College, which still has parts of the old city wall, are particularly important ones. The Museum of Oxford in St Aldates has a very good section on the Civil War in Oxford.

Outside the city, you can visit Broughton Castle near Banbury. This has changed little since the days when Lord Saye and Sele lived there, and the present family are direct descendants. Half way between Oxford and Banbury is Rousham House, which was a Royalist stronghold.

Acknowledgements

The authors and publishers are grateful to the following for permission to reproduce material:

The Ashmolean Museum, page 23; BBC Hulton Picture Library, page 34; the Bodleian Library, pages 6, 7, 26, 47 (from Arch. Antiq. A.11.13), page 22 (from [E] C.17:70 Oxf [98]), page 28 (from 80.A29.ART.BS), page 33 (from MS.ADD.D.114), page 42 (from MS.CLAR.91), pages 25 and 29; the Trustees of the British Museum, page 37; the British Library, pages 16, 17, 20, 40 and 41; the Chatsworth Settlement Trustees, Devonshire Collection, Chatsworth, page 31; Greater London Council as Trustees of the Iveagh Bequest, Kenwood, page 30; Lord Saye and Sele, Broughton Castle, Oxon, page 5; Macmillan, London and Basingstoke, pages 11 and 12; Mary Evans Picture Library, pages 35 and 39; National Galleries of Scotland, page 28; National Portrait Gallery, London, pages 7, 27, 30, 39, 41, 44 and 45; the National Trust, page 29; the National War Museum, page 20; Oxfordshire County Council, pages 8, 27, 32 and 50; the Tabley Collection, University of Manchester, page 5; Mr N H L Temple, page 9; Valence House Museum, London Borough of Barking and Dagenham, page 38. The painting on page 4 is reproduced by gracious permission of Her Majesty the Queen.

Every attempt has been made to contact copyright holders, but we apologise if any have been overlooked.

Index

Page references in **bold** print are illustrations.

Abingdon 18, 28,36,38
artillery 20
Astley, Sir Jacob 24
Aston, Sir Arthur 30,34
Aulicus *see* Mercurius Aulicus

Banbury 18, 24
Bernini 4
Birkenhead, John *see* Mercurius Aulicus
Bodleian Library 6,46
Bodley, Sir Thomas 6
Brasenose College 23
Bristol 14,31,37,44
Broughton Castle 11, 18
Buckingham 18,41
Bullingdon Green 40,41
Burford 40
Byron, Sir John **5,**11,30

Carfax 34
Caernarvon, Earl of 24
Castle, Oxford 34
Cavaliers, definition of 3
Cave, Walter 11,38
Charles, Prince 15,**28,**37,44
Cherwell, river 26,41,42
Christ Church 15,24,25,**26,**27,28,43
City, Council 9–11,15,35,45
   Trades 10
Clarendon, Earl of *see* Hyde
coins 23
Convocation House **50**
Cornmarket 20
Council *see* city
Cowley 40,42
Croke, Unton 38,43,46
Cromwell 3,31,40–2,45

De Gomme *see* Gomme
disease 34
Dobson, William 32,45

Edgehill, Battle of **12**,13,15
Elsfield 42
Essex, Earl of 31,40,41
Exeter 31
Eynsham 40

Fairfax, Sir Thomas 3,14,15,27,**41**–5
Falkland, Lord 30,**31**
Fanshawe, Anne 37,38
   Sir Richard 37,**38**
fire 35

Forth, Earl of 30
Frewin Hall 20

Gaunt House 18, 41
Gloucester 31
Gloucester Hall 20
Godstow 20
Gomme, Sir Bernard de 17
guns 20

Headington 41–3
Heath, Edward 33,38
   Lucy and family 38,39
Henrietta Maria 3,4,8,**27,**28,29,44
Heydon, Sir John 40
Hopton, Sir Ralph 31
Hull 14,31
Hyde, Edward **30,**42,45

Irish 14,40
Islip 18,40

James, Duke of York 15,28,44

Kettell, Dr 12

Laud, Archbishop 3,**7,**8,9
Legge, General 30
Le Sueur 8,27
Lostwithiel 41

Magdalen, College 40,45
   Bridge 12,41,42
   Grove 20
Marston 38,41–3,46
Marston Moor, Battle of 40
Maurice, Prince 15,31,44
Mercurius Aulicus 24,25,40
Mercurius Britanicus 25
Merton College **7,27,**28
Mint, The Royal 23

Naseby, Battle of 44
Newark 40
Newbridge 40
Newbury, Battle of 30,31
Newcastle, Earl of 14,31
New College 12,20
New Inn Hall 23,35
Newport Pagnell 31
Nixon, John 15,45
Nottingham 14

Osney 20

Papists 3,9
Pennyman, Sir William 34
Percy, Lord 30
Pink, Dr 12
Plymouth 31
prisoners of war 34
propaganda 2,24,38
punishment 33
Puritans 3,7,9

Queen *see* Henrietta Maria

Richmond, Duke of **30,**31
Rockingham Castle 39
Roundheads, definition of 3
Rupert, Prince 8,15,25,28,**29,**30,31,33, 40,41,44,**45**

St Clements 40,43
St Johns College **8,**23,38
St Marys Church **9,**12
Sandford 40
Savile 14
Saye and Sele, Lord **5,**12,15
Schools, The 20
Scots 40,42
Shotover 20
Smyth, John 11,38
Stokes, William 28
Sueur *see* Le Sueur

Taylor, John **25,**34
Thames, River 25,26,40
Trinity College 12
Turnham Green 16

University 6–8,12,15,24,45

Van Dyck 4

Wadham College **6**
Waller, Sir William 40
Winceby, Battle of 31
Witney 40
Wolvercote 20,24,25,30,40
Wood, Anthony 9,11,12,15,23,24,34, 35,36,45,47
Woodstock 28,40

York 14,40
York, Duke of *see* James

A World of Change

This book is part of a series entitled A *World of Change*, intended for the 11–14 age group. The aim of the whole series is to combine a firm framework of historical fact with a 'skill-based' approach. The factual content provides continuity, and the opportunity to study causation and development. It is balanced by the two other vital ingredients for lively study of history: opportunity for 'empathy', which enables children to make an imaginative leap into the past; and study of a variety of original sources, both written and visual.

The series comprises a core textbook which studies a number of themes important in the Early Modern Age, approximately 1450–1700; a number of linked topic books; and a teacher's book for the whole series (which includes copyright-free worksheets).

The core book is primarily concerned with the British Isles, but within the context of what was happening in the rest of the world, known and unknown. The well-known political, religious and economic themes are considered. So too are the lives of ordinary men, women and children, and the way in which both change and continuity affected them. The book does not set out to be a full chronological survey, but it is hoped that it is sufficiently flexible to be used in that way if desired.

The core textbook is complete in itself, but has also been designed to provide a number of stepping-off points for 'patch studies'. Opportunities for this kind of work are provided by the eight *World of Change* topic books which are clearly linked to the themes in the main book. However, the topic books are also designed so that they can be used on their own if desired. All the topic books are listed on the back cover.

For the teacher

The use of original sources can present some problems at this level. We have tried to minimise this by careful selection and use of glosses and linking paraphrase where necessary. Further consideration of the use of original source material in the classroom can be found in the Teacher's Book which accompanies the whole *World of Change* series. Suggestions on the use of this book can also be found there.

Some suggestions for useful background reading:

Andrew Carter and John Stevenson, *The Oxfordshire Area in the Civil War* (BBC Radio Oxford Publication, 1974)

Andrew Clark (ed.), *The Life and Times of Anthony Wood* (Wishart and Co., 1932)

Ruth Fasnacht, *A History of the City of Oxford* (Basil Blackwell, 1954)

Margaret Toynbee and Peter Young, *Strangers in Oxford* (Phillimore, 1973)

Victoria County History, Vol. 3, 1954

C.V. Wedgwood, *The King's War* (Penguin, 1983)

© Tony and Rosemary Kelly 1987

All rights reserved. No part of this publication may be reproduced, stored in a retrieval system or transmitted in any form or by any means, electronic, mechanical, photocopying, recording or otherwise, without the prior written consent of the copyright holders. Applications for such permission should be addressed to the publishers: Stanley Thornes (Publishers) Ltd, Old Station Drive, Leckhampton, CHELTENHAM GL53 0DN, England

First published in 1987 by:
Stanley Thornes (Publishers) Ltd
Old Station Drive
Leckhampton
CHELTENHAM GL53 0DN
England

Typeset by Gedset Ltd, Cheltenham
in 11/13 Optima Light and 11/12 Goudy
Printed and bound in Great Britain by
Ebenezer Baylis & Son, Worcester

British Library Cataloguing in Publication Data
Kelly, Rosemary
   A city at war : Oxford 1642-1646. — (World
of change topic books)
   1. Oxford (Oxfordshire) — Social life and
customs
   I. Title II. Kelly, Tony III. Series
   942.5'74062   DA690.09

ISBN 0-85950-540-5